TWENTIETH-CENTURY
DEFENCES
IN WARWICKSHIRE

TWENTIETH-CENTURY DEFENCES
IN WARWICKSHIRE

STEVE CARVELL

TEMPUS

Front cover illustrations
Main picture: Type 24 pillbox at former RAF Stratford (PB37, June 2006).
Inset: Mushroom type pillbox at former RAF Long Marston (PB33, June 2003).

Back cover illustration
Utility build communal buildings at former RAF Long Marston (AB29, June 2006).

First published 2007

Tempus Publishing Limited
The Mill, Brimscombe Port,
Stroud, Gloucestershire, GL5 2QG
www.tempus-publishing.com

© Steve Carvell, 2007

The right of Steve Carvell to be identified as the Author
of this work has been asserted in accordance with the
Copyrights, Designs and Patents Act 1988.

British Library Cataloguing in Publication Data.
A catalogue record for this book is available from the British Library.

ISBN 978 07524 4268 6

Typesetting and origination by Tempus Publishing Limited.
Printed in Great Britain.

Contents

Acknowledgements

My grateful thanks to the following organisations and people: Warwickshire County Council, Historic Environment Records Office (formerly Sites and Monuments Records Office); Warwickshire County Council, County Archives Office; Warwickshire County Council, County Reference Library; members of the Pillbox Study Group (PSG) and the Fortress Study Group (FSG), with particular thanks to Graham Matthews, Alistair Graham Kerr, Adrian Armishaw, Bernard Lowry, Mike Osborne, Martin Mace and Charles Blackwood. Thanks are also due to the Council for British Archaeology (CBA); Will Jarman of Air Atlantique Classic Flight for the tour of Coventry Airport (former RAF Baginton) and for permission to photograph the buildings and classic aircraft; Gamecock Barracks MoD staff for the tour of the site and their permission to photograph buildings; Ford Land Rover for photographs of RAF Gaydon; the *Leamington Times* newspaper for photographs of RAF Gaydon; Warwickshire landowners and farmers for permission to visit defence sites; Amy Rigg at Tempus Publishing; and my wife Janet for her patience and help.

Introduction

The intention of this book is to provide a guide to, and record of, the buildings and structures in Warwickshire associated with the defence of the nation against the many threats of the twentieth century. The coverage is not comprehensive but, nevertheless, it does provide samples of a broad range of the twentieth-century defences built in the county.

This book does not cover the political and human aspects; but tribute must be paid to the armed forces and civilians who endured two world wars and other armed conflicts during a particularly turbulent century. In common with all counties, Warwickshire has numerous war memorials and graves commemorating the many people who died in their country's service.

Until recent years, the study and recording of buildings and structures associated with twentieth-century defences has received relatively little attention. However, the Defence of Britain Project was instigated to survey and record twentieth-century defences in Britain following a trial survey untaken by the Fortress Study Group (FSG). The survey was coordinated by the Council for British Archaeology (CBA) and supported by national study groups and council sites and monuments departments. The survey was undertaken between 1995 and 2002. Volunteers and members of research groups such as the Fortress Study Group (FSG), Pillbox Study Group (PSG) and Airfield Research Group (ARG) undertook a lot of the work. The database results of the survey are available for viewing on the Council for British Archaeology (CBA) website.

Demolition of Second World War defences commenced before the end of the conflict, when the risk of Nazi invasion had diminished. However, the demolition of these and Cold War defences is ongoing today. Despite the extent of the demolition work many examples of defence installations and structures survive throughout Great Britain. The extent of twentieth-century defences in Warwickshire is not numerous compared to counties with coastal regions and those on the east side of Great Britain. Within Warwickshire a wide variety of defence buildings and structures still survive, but are at risk of future demolition. For many people twentieth-century defences are considered to be unsightly eyesores and unwanted reminders of wars and conflicts. But it is important that these defences be recorded for the benefit of future historians and archaeologists, and in some instances preservation of key examples should be considered.

Within Warwickshire very few defence structures associated with the First World War survive, with the exception of the buildings used for drill halls and recruitment centres. This book concentrates principally on examples of surviving structures from the Second World War and Cold War periods.

Following the creation of West Midlands Metropolitan Council in 1974 the Warwickshire County boundary was altered, thus Birmingham and Coventry were no longer inside the Warwickshire County boundary. Within the West Midlands Metropolitan borough many of the twentieth-century defences have been demolished, and so this book mainly concentrates on surviving defences in the post-1974 Warwickshire county boundary.

Many of the defence sites are on private farmland and so are not readily accessible, but in most cases they can still be viewed from a distance from public footpaths, canal towpaths and public roads. The general public must not trespass onto private land without permission.

Many of the structures built for defence purposes are derelict and should not be entered They are often structurally unsafe and can contain dangerous materials like asbestos and broken glass. The recommendation is not to enter derelict buildings and structures.

1

Second World War Stop Line Defences and Pillboxes

Introduction

Following the May–June 1940, evacuation of Allied forces from Dunkirk and the defeat of France, Britain prepared itself to repel what was thought to be an imminent German invasion. On 16 July 1940, Hitler issued Directive No.16, stating that an invasion was necessary 'to eliminate the English homeland as a base for carrying on the war against Germany, and, should it be necessary, to occupy completely'. The German code-name for the invasion of Britain was Operation Sealion. To counter the potential invasion, extensive fortifications were rapidly constructed during 1940, comprising mainly coastal defences and a network of inland stop lines. The stop lines consisted of natural and artificial barriers, particularly rivers and canals, backed by defences of, for example, anti-tank ditches, barbed wire entanglements, roadblocks, weapon positions, pillboxes and other obstacles.

The land defence of Great Britain was divided into five main regional army commands: eastern (including London), southern, western (including Wales), northern and Scottish. Stop line defences were planned in all of these army command regions. Warwickshire was within the western command region with the county boundary bordering the southern and northern command regions.

Within Warwickshire the following stop line defences were planned:

> Southern Command Oxford Canal Stop Line
> Western Command River Avon Stop Line
> Western Command Napton to Coventry Stop Line
> Western Command Coventry to Tamworth Stop Line
> Western Command Stratford to Tamworth Stop Line
> Western Command Droitwich to Watling Street Stop Line

The routes of the above stop lines through Warwickshire can be relatively easily traced as they generally follow the routes of rivers and canals. Many of the artificial defence structures associated with these stop lines were removed towards the end of, and immediately after, the Second World War. However, pillboxes and anti-tank concrete blocks still survive in Warwickshire.

The main types of pillboxes constructed at Warwickshire stop lines were standard types 22 and 24. These were two of seven standard designs supplied during June and July 1940 by the FW3 branch of the Directorate of Fortifications and Works at the War Office. The construction code types were FW/22 to FW/28, or abbreviated to types 22 to 28.

Within Warwickshire a number of Stent prefabricated pillboxes survive. The size and plan shape of these pillboxes is similar to the FW3/26 design. The Stent pillbox is made up of pre-cast concrete inner and outer panels secured between vertical concrete posts with the cavity filled with concrete. Roof construction consisted of precast panels with a covering of concrete poured on site. The name Stent prefabricated pillbox derived from the manufacturer, Stent Precast Concrete Ltd.

(Refer to Appendix 1, Warwickshire Pillbox Types for a summary and comparison of the pillbox types.)

The majority of pillbox types 22 to 28 were constructed during 1940 when a German invasion was considered to be close. Following the Battle of Britain, in which the RAF fought off the Luftwaffe, Operation Sealion was postponed on 12 October 1940 until the summer of 1941, by which time the German invasion of Russia made an offensive on Britain unlikely. By September 1941 pillboxes were only being built for special purposes, and by February 1942 the Commander-in-Chief directed that no more pillboxes be built. Estimates indicate that up to 28,000 pillboxes may have been constructed throughout Britain.

The following pages describe the Warwickshire stop line defences and associated pillboxes.

Southern Command Oxford Canal Stop Line

(Claydon to Warwick Section)

The General Headquarters Anti-Tank Stop Line (GHQ Line) was constructed during 1940 to protect London and the industrial hinterland from the advances of a German invasion. One section of the GHQ Line was the GHQ Red Line between Reading and Malmesbury, generally following the course of the river Thames. The intention was to block the main communication routes heading north over the Thames between the Cotswolds and the Chilterns, and thus provide an extra layer of protection for the Midlands.

From the GHQ Red Line near Abingdon, the Southern Command Oxford Canal Stop Line followed the course of the Thames to Oxford, then the Oxford Canal via Banbury to Napton-on-the-Hill, and thence west along the Grand Union Canal to the river Avon between Leamington Spa and Warwick. The Oxford Canal Stop Line crosses the Warwickshire county boundary near Claydon, north of Banbury. The intended purpose of this stop line was to protect the industrial Midlands from potential German advances. The Oxford Canal Stop Line was never fully developed, and the construction of the line was generally abandoned during late 1940 when many stop lines were declared obsolete. (The Southern Command Oxford Canal Stop Line was also known as the Southern Command Oxford and Grand Union Canals Stop Line.)

The following are examples of pillboxes in Warwickshire on the Southern Command Oxford Canal Stop Line:

PB01 Stent prefabricated pillbox near Priors Hardwick (NGR: SP 458458)
This pillbox is located on the west bank of the Oxford Canal, WNW of Stoneton Moat Farm, near Priors Hardwick. It is of standard Stent prefabricated concrete construction, and while the condition of the pillbox itself is fair, it is considerably overgrown with ivy and encircled by bushes.

PB02 Stent prefabricated pillbox near Priors Hardwick (NGR: SP 462565)

Situated on the east bank of the Oxford Canal, near bridge 122 close to Priors Hardwick. It is standard Stent prefabricated concrete construction. As a point of interest, it appears that the builder has installed some of the main vertical prefabricated panels back to front! The pillbox condition is fair but there is ground subsidence and a hole in the roof.

PB03 Stent prefabricated pillbox near Napton-on-the-Hill (NGR: SP 459596)

Located on the east bank of the Oxford Canal near bridge 116, Holt Farm, near Napton-on-the-Hill. Standard Stent prefabricated concrete construction.

PB04 Stent prefabricated pillbox near Napton-on-the-Hill (NGR: SP 458603)

Located on the east bank of the Oxford Canal this example of the type provided protection to canal locks. It is of standard Stent prefabricated concrete construction. The door and embrasures have been sealed with blockwork and brickwork.

PB05 and PB06 Type 22 pillboxes by the Grand Union Canal

Both PB05, near Stockton (NGR: SP 433648), and PB06, near Bascote (NGR: SP 381639), have been destroyed.

PB02 Stent pillbox near Priors Hardwick (July 2003).

PB03 Stent pillbox near Napton-on-the-Hill (July 2003).

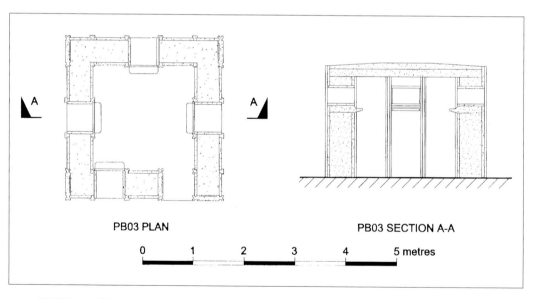

PB03 Stent pillbox near Napton-on-the-Hill: plan and section.

PB04 Stent pillbox near Napton-on-the-Hill (March 2006).

PB07 Type 24 pillbox near Radford Semele (NGR: SP 353649)

Found by Radford Bottom Lock, near Grand Union Canal bridge 34. This pillbox protected the Grand Union Canal locks and the former London Midland & Scottish Railway (LM&SR) viaduct crossing the canal. The pillbox is positioned on the dismantled railway embankment to the west of the viaduct. The entrance door faces the dismantled railway line and the main embrasures face the canal locks and viaduct.

The pillbox is of standard type 24 irregular hexagon design. The entrance door face has two rifle embrasures and the other five wall faces each have one embrasure. The wall construction is brickwork shuttering with concrete infill and an overall wall thickness of 450mm. The roof is reinforced concrete construction. Internally there is a 225mm thick brickwork Y-shaped blast/anti-ricochet wall. Anti-ricochet timber exists on parts of the ceiling and walls. The entrance has a low-level drop-down steel bar grille with internal latch.

PB08 Pillbox near Radford Semele (NGR: SP 339649)

This particular example was demolished during the 1950s. It was originally located by the Grand Union Canal west of bridge 34.

PB07 Type 24 pillbox near Radford Semele (July 2003).

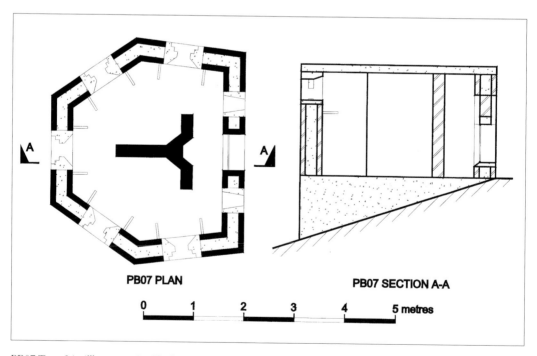

PB07 Type 24 pillbox near Radford Semele: plan and section.

Western Command Avon Stop Line

(Bidford-on-Avon to Coventry Section)

The Western Command Avon Stop Line route started from the Bristol Channel and followed the river Severn to Tewkesbury; from Tewkesbury it carried on along the river Avon to near Coventry. The section of this stop line that enters Warwickshire runs from Bidford-on-Avon to Coventry. Its intended purpose was to form a barrier to block advances either from the east towards Wales and the north-west Midlands, or from south Wales towards Bristol and south-east England. Very few defences survive along the Warwickshire section of the Western Command Avon Stop Line, but good examples of defences survive in the Worcestershire section at Offenham Ford (pillbox), Pershore (bridge defences) and Eckington Bridge (pillbox).

Examples of pillboxes in Warwickshire on the Western Command Avon Stop Line include:

PB09 Type 22 pillbox at Warwick (NGR: SP 298654)

This pillbox protected the railway viaduct crossing the river Avon at Warwick. The pillbox was constructed at the top of the embankment on the north side of the river Avon. Access to the pillbox was from low level on the embankment via a vertical, steel rung cat ladder located between brickwork buttress support walls. Unfortunately, the pillbox was demolished during 2002.

Above: PB09 Type 22 pillbox at Warwick (December 2001).

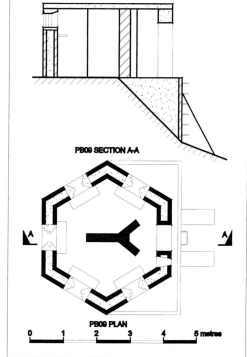

Right: PB09 Type 22 pillbox at Warwick: plan and section (based on photographs).

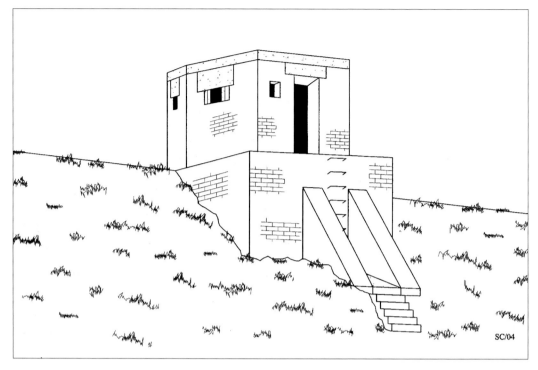

SC/04

PB09 Type 22 pillbox at Warwick. This is a sketch view *c.*1941 (based on photographs).

PB10 Pillbox near Sherbourne, Warwick (NGR: SP 267610)

This (since demolished) pillbox was located on the north-west approach to the Sherbourne to Barford Bridge over the river Avon. It was built on the embankment between the bridge and the flood relief channel.

Western Command Napton to Coventry Stop Line

This stop line followed the route of the Oxford Canal from Napton-on-the-Hill via Rugby to Coventry, joining the Coventry canal north of the city. The line was not fully developed, but anti-tank obstacles were erected at many of the canal bridges. The Home Guard provided infantry to guard the bridges. The one surviving pillbox on this stop line is at Clifton upon Dunsmore.

PB21 Stent prefabricated pillbox at Clifton upon Dunsmore (NGR: SP 523758)

This pillbox is located on the south bank of the Oxford Canal near bridge 66, Clifton upon Dunsmore, Rugby. It is of standard Stent prefabricated concrete construction. The pillbox has stepped anti-ricochet embrasures constructed of prefabricated concrete.

PB21 Stent pillbox at Clifton upon Dunsmore (July 2003).

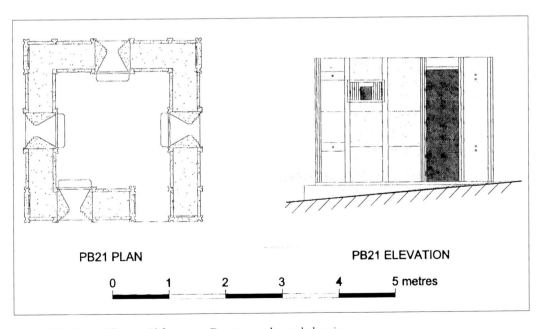

PB21 Stent pillbox at Clifton upon Dunsmore: plan and elevation.

Western Command Coventry to Tamworth Stop Line

This proposed stop line route started from Coventry and headed north following the route of the Coventry Canal and then north-west to join the Tamworth to Ashbourne stop line at the river Tame near Tamworth. One surviving pillbox on this stop line is located at Alvecote Priory.

PB25 Pillbox at Alvecote Priory (NGR: SK251043)
This example is located on the south bank of the Coventry Canal near bridge 59, at Alvecote Priory, 1.5 miles north-west of Polesworth and 0.25 miles from the Warwickshire/Staffordshire county boundary. The pillbox was originally the dovecote for Alvecote Priory and was adapted for use as a pillbox around 1940. It has a flat reinforced concrete roof and stonewalls.

Western Command Stratford to Tamworth Stop Line

This proposed stop line route was from the river Avon at Stratford heading north, passing to the west of Coventry and joining with the Tamworth to Ashbourne stop line near Tamworth, Staffordshire. The Stratford to Tamworth stop line was not developed. Natural and artificial barriers on the route that may have been used for defences include sections of the Stratford Canal, the river Blythe and the river Tame. Tamworth was a designated anti-tank island and Second World War defences survive near Tamworth within Staffordshire.

PB25 Pillbox at Alvecote Priory (October 2006).

Western Command Droitwich to Watling Street Stop Line

The Western Command Droitwich to Watling Street stop line was a proposed additional stop line to defend Birmingham and Coventry from the south. The proposed stop line route was to start from the river Severn and run to Watling Street at the boundary of the Western and Northern Commands. The stop line would have run from the river Severn at Upper Arley, north of Bewdley, down river to the Droitwich Canal, proceeded overland to the river Avon at Binton and then along the river Avon to Stratford-upon-Avon. It would then have followed the river Avon to Warwick/Leamington Spa, run alongside the LM&S Railway line to Rugby and then the river Swift to Watling Street. This proposed stop line was not developed but anti-tank blocks do survive at bridges on the stop line route. (ATB03 and ATB04)

(Reference: Public Records Office, Kew – WO 199/1800/20 dated 27.06.1940)

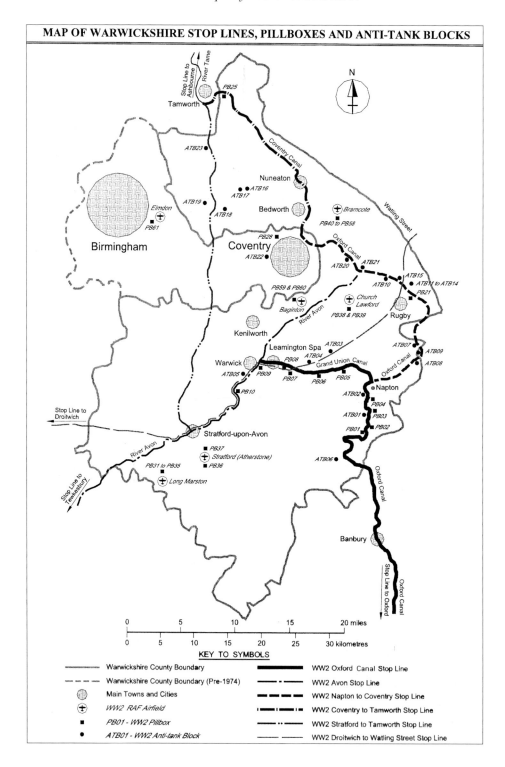

MAP OF WARWICKSHIRE STOP LINES, PILLBOXES AND ANTI-TANK BLOCKS

KEY TO SYMBOLS

Warwickshire County Boundary	WW2 Oxford Canal Stop Line
Warwickshire County Boundary (Pre-1974)	WW2 Avon Stop Line
Main Towns and Cities	WW2 Napton to Coventry Stop Line
WW2 RAF Airfield	WW2 Coventry to Tamworth Stop Line
PB01 - WW2 Pillbox	WW2 Stratford to Tamworth Stop Line
ATB01 - WW2 Anti-tank Block	WW2 Droitwich to Watling Street Stop Line

2

Second World War Anti-Tank Islands and Anti-Tank Obstacles

Introduction

The planning and construction of the stop lines was generally abandoned during late 1940, when many stop lines were declared obsolete. This followed the replacement of General Ironside by General Brooke in July 1940. After this appointment the defence strategy was switched to defence in depth and a more aggressive and mobile form of counter-attack. Mobile forces were located near to the coastal defences, and fortified inland towns and villages were created. The fortified towns and villages were given various designations, such as anti-tank islands, nodal points, centres of resistance, and defended localities. The designation depended on the defence requirements and the strength of defences, which were designed to obstruct the progress of the invader, and would be constructed around the complete perimeter of the settlement in question.

The Warwickshire towns of Henley-in-Arden, Stratford-upon-Avon, Warwick and Leamington Spa, Rugby and the city of Coventry were proposed as anti-tank islands, and were defended by the Home Guard.

Some of the main artificial defences for both anti-tank islands and anti-tank stop lines were anti-tank obstacles. The purpose of the anti-tank obstacles was to obstruct the progress of a tank, or, should it attempt to cross the obstacle, expose the tank's vulnerable underside to fire. A summary of the main types of artificial anti-tank obstacles built during the Second World War is provided below:

1. **Anti-tank concrete blocks** – Constructed to various different designs, for example, cube, coffin, pimple, cylinder and octagonal. They were positioned in lines or groups to form a continuous anti-tank barrier.
2. **Anti-tank walls** – These were concrete walls built as a continuous barrier.
3. **Anti-tank vertical rails** – Sections of rolled steel joist (RSJ) were installed vertically in concrete blocks or in sockets in a road to form a barrier.
4. **Anti-tank horizontal rails** – Sections of RSJ were installed horizontally between concrete blocks cast with slots.
5. **Anti-tank hairpins** – Bent sections of RSJ were installed in sockets in a road to form a barrier.

6. **Anti-tank ditches** – These were artificially dug trenches designed to impede the progress of tanks and vehicles.

A combination of the above obstacles was often used to construct a roadblock alongside pillboxes, defended buildings, trenches, weapons pits, mines, loop-holed walls and barbed wire.

One example of an anti-tank island pillbox (PB28) survives adjacent to the minor road to Keresley on the north side of Coventry. The pillbox is square in plan with a single embrasure facing north. Construction is made up of brick walls and a reinforced concrete roof.

The Warwickshire anti-tank stop lines utilised rivers and canals as tank obstacles. The bridges crossing these rivers and canals would have been defended, and in many instances anti-tank obstacles would have been positioned at the bridges.

The following are examples of surviving anti-tank blocks in Warwickshire. The majority of these examples formed part of the defences for the main anti-tank stop lines. The 'octagonal' concrete blocks with an octagonal section are a relatively rare type of block that was not distributed nationally. The standard dimensions were 1040mm high x 1400mm wide across sides x 300mm-diameter central hole. Timber battens were attached to small apertures in the sides of the blocks to assist in manoeuvring the blocks into position.

Warwickshire Anti-Tank Blocks

ATB01 Octagonal blocks at Oxford Canal bridge 116, Napton (NGR: SP 459594)
Two octagonal concrete blocks are located on either side of the west approach ramp to Oxford Canal bridge 116, near Napton-on-the-Hill.

ATB01 Octagonal block at Oxford Canal bridge 116 (July 2003).

ATB02 Octagonal blocks at Oxford Canal bridge 114 (July 2003).

ATB03 Octagonal blocks near Offchurch (August 2003).

ATB02 Octagonal blocks at Oxford Canal bridge 114, Napton (NGR: SP 457604)

Two octagonal concrete blocks are located adjacent to the west approach ramp to Oxford Canal bridge 114, near Napton-on-the-Hill. Several timber battens are attached to the blocks.

ATB03 Octagonal blocks near Offchurch (NGR: SP 382666)

Two octagonal concrete blocks are located adjacent to the north exit from the road bridge over the disused former LM&S Railway between Leamington Spa and Rugby. The railway cutting is particularly deep at this location and would have provided a formidable obstacle to tanks; however, the cutting is only about 0.5 miles long and would have been relatively easy to bypass. The road is unclassified and the single-track (5300mm-wide) bridge is approximately 1.5 miles from the Grand Union Canal. The condition of one block is fair, whereas another is broken into two fragments.

ATB03 Octagonal blocks near Offchurch (August 2003). View of the bridge from the east.

ATB04 Octagonal block near Offchurch (October 2003). Since 2003 the disused railway bridge has been demolished; however, ATB04 survives.

ATB04 Octagonal block at disused railway near Offchurch (NGR: SP 359651)

One octagonal concrete block is located by the dismantled LM&S railway, approximately 0.25 miles from the Grand Union Canal. The LM&S railway between Leamington Spa and Rugby was part of the proposed Droitwich to Watling Street stop line.

The block was initially cast with a matrix of five 225mm holes; four of these holes were infilled, with concrete leaving one central hole.

ATB05 Octagonal blocks at Leafield Bridge near Warwick (NGR: SP 280631)

Two octagonal concrete blocks are located on strictly private land at Leafield Bridge over the river Avon, Lodge Wood, near Warwick. One block is located adjacent to the southern approach ramp and the other block is located next to the northern approach ramp. The bridge is a single-track (3800mm-wide) private bridge.

ATB06 Cylinders near Fenny Compton (NGR: SP 432534)

Six concrete cylinders are located by the gateway to a disused garage site, by Wormleighton Road, near the junction with the A423 (T) road. The cylinders may originally have been located at the nearby Oxford Canal bridges.

ATB06 Cylinders near Fenny Compton (March 2006).

AB07 Cylinders on south side of the A45 near Willoughby (August 2003).

AB07 Cylinders on the north side of the A45 near Willoughby (August 2003).

ATB07 Cylinders in the café car park near Willoughby (August 2003).

ATB07 Cylinders near Willoughby (NGR: SP 525674)

Three concrete cylinders (painted red) are to be found on the south side of the A45, opposite a garage with six concrete cylinders on the north side in front of a garage and café. In addition, there are in excess of twenty concrete cylinders randomly placed by the car park to the rear of the café. The cylinders were probably originally located at the numerous bridges crossing the nearby Oxford Canal.

ATB08 Cylinders at Wolfhamcote Hall near Braunston (NGR: SP 526653)

Four concrete cylinders are positioned at the entrance road to Wolfhamcote Hall. The cylinders were probably originally located at the nearby bridges crossing the Oxford Canal.

ATB09 Cylinders at Oxford Canal bridge near Braunston (NGR: SP 526653)

Two concrete cylinders are located in the hedge adjacent to Oxford Canal bridge 95 near Braunston.

ATB10 Pimples at Newbold-on-Avon near Rugby (NGR: SP 488773)

In excess of ten concrete pimples are located adjacent to the B4112 road. They probably formed a continuous row of pimples from the road to the Oxford Canal bridge 50. A post-war change to ground level has concealed more pimples. Three pimples are located adjacent to the Oxford Canal bridge 50 but are concealed by vegetation.

ATB08 Cylinders at Wolfhamcote Hall near Braunston (August 2003).

ATB11–ATB14 Cylinders and rail cubes at Brownsover Lane, Rugby (NGR: Various)

Brownsover Lane was formerly one of the main roads heading north from Rugby to Lutterworth, and is now bypassed by the A426 dual carriageway. An interesting connection with the Second World War is the Brownsover Hotel, adjacent to Brownsover Lane. For several years the building was the headquarters for Sir Frank Whittle's design team which worked on developing the jet engine.

The following anti-tank cylinders and cubes exist (2004) alongside Brownsover Lane. Each cylinder is engraved on one end with a letter 'R'.

ATB11 (NGR: SP 511778): Five concrete cylinders randomly located in the undergrowth near the dual carriageway roundabout.

ATB12 (NGR: SP 510776): Four 600mm concrete cubes, each with a single vertical railway line projection. Blocks randomly located in the corner of a field.

ATB13 (NGR: SP 509776): Ten concrete cylinders stacked horizontally adjacent to a disused gateway adjacent to the Brownsover Hotel. Eight are 900mm high x 600mm diameter and two are 600mm high x 600mm diameter.

ATB14 (NGR: SP 508775): One concrete cylinder adjacent to the boundary of the Brownsover Hotel. The cylinder size is 900mm high x 600mm diameter.

ATB15 Pimples at Old Leicester Road, Rugby (NGR: SP 503771)

Fifteen truncated anti-tank pimples are positioned adjacent to the road tunnel passing under the Oxford Canal. Ten are located on the west side of the road and five on the east side. Each pimple has a 900mm square base with sloping sides to a 300mm square top. The overall height is 950mm.

ATB16 Cylinders at Old Arley (NGR: SP 279905)

Six concrete cylinders, each positioned vertically to form an ornamental crescent on a lawn. Each cylinder is capped with a modern concrete-domed disc to give the appearance of saddle stones.

ATB17 Cylinders at Devitts Green (NGR: SP 274903)

In excess of 200 concrete cylinders are vertically double-stacked to provide a boundary wall to a farmhouse. The cylinders would have been procured from numerous different roadblock locations throughout Warwickshire. There are two sizes of cylinder 900mm high x 600mm diameter, and 600mm high x 600mm diameter. The 'cylinder wall' is capped with in situ concrete.

ATB18 Cylinders and cube at Green End near Fillongley (NGR: SP 260864)

Three concrete cylinders and one concrete cube are located on a grass verge in front of a factory at Green End, 1.5 miles west of Fillongley.

ATB19 Cylinders near Maxstoke (NGR: SP 232881)

Two concrete cylinders are located on a grass verge, Fillongley Road, 1 mile north of Maxstoke.

ATB15 Anti-tank pimples at Old Leicester Road, Rugby (September 2004).

ATB17 Anti-tank cylinders at Devitts Green (September 2004).

ATB22 Cubes at Tile Hill Lane, Coventry (May 2006).

ATB20 Cylinders near Easenhall (NGR: SP 458787)

Six 600mm-diameter concrete cylinders south-west of Easenhall on the southern approach to Oxford Canal bridge 37. Each cylinder is engraved on one end with a letter 'R'.

ATB21 Cylinders near Harborough Magna (NGR: SP 468784)

Eight 600mm-diameter concrete cylinders by the southern approach to Oxford Canal bridge 42 are partially concealed by rubble and a hedge. Also, one concrete cylinder is located by the nearby railway footbridge (NGR: SP 4687782) and one cylinder on the opposite side of the railway where the footpath meets the road (NGR: SP 468784). The latter two cylinders were probably originally positioned at the canal bridge.

ATB22 Cubes at Tile Hill Lane, Coventry (NGR: SP 277782)

Four concrete cubes are located adjacent to the junction of Tile Hill Lane (B4101) and Banner Lane, Tile Hill, Coventry. They are the surviving remains of a roadblock that may have formed part of the Coventry anti-tank island defences.

ATB23 Cylinder at River Tame near Kingsbury (NGR: SP 213962)

One 600mm-diameter concrete cylinder by the river Tame footbridge near Kingsbury.

3

RAF Airfields and Buildings

Introduction

Airfields 1900 to 1933

One of the earliest military airfields in Warwickshire was at Castle Bromwich. The Midland Aero Club established the airfield in May 1912. In May 1915 the Royal Flying Corps No.5 Reserve Squadron was based at the Castle Bromwich Airfield. Following a German Zeppelin air raid on Birmingham in January 1916, No.5 Squadron was given the task of defending the city against the Zeppelins, but the squadron was not suitably equipped to attack high-flying airships. During June and July 1916, Nos 28 and 38 Squadrons were formed at Castle Bromwich and assumed responsibility for defence against Zeppelin raids. The last major Zeppelin raid on Warwickshire occurred on 12 April 1918, when a Zeppelin dropped bombs south of Coventry and south-west of Birmingham.

Lilbourne Airfield near Rugby was originally used during 1913 and was brought back into service in June 1916 when three fighters from No.5 Squadron were based there for the defence of Coventry against Zeppelin raids. The airfield closed in 1919.

In Coventry a new airfield was opened at Radford during 1917. The airfield was designated No.1 Aircraft Acceptance Park and handled hundreds of aircraft produced at factories in Coventry. The Siddeley Deasy factory at Parkside, Coventry, built over 1,000 RE7 and RE8 aircraft.

During 1918 an airfield was constructed at Whitley, Coventry, and used for storage. Landing grounds were used at Meriden and Knowle during the First World War.

Following the end of the First World War, many squadrons were disbanded and the Warwickshire Aircraft Acceptance Parks at Castle Bromwich and Radford were closed. The Air Ministry acquired Castle Bromwich Airfield in August 1918 and licensed it for civil flying. By the end of 1918 the airfield was equipped with over twenty sheds for storage purposes and nine large sheds for aircraft. During 1926, No.605 County of Warwick Squadron was formed at Castle Bromwich. The squadron acted as a reserve for the regular RAF squadrons.

In 1920 the Armstong-Whitworth Aircraft Co. bought the Whitley Airfield. Armstrong-Whitworth initially manufactured the 'Siskin' aircraft that was the first all-metal frame fighter aircraft to be flown by the RAF.

There are no known surviving airfield buildings from the 1900–1933 era at either Castle Bromwich or Radford.

Airfields 1934 to 1939: the Expansion Period

The early 1930s was a period of growth in civil aviation and new municipal aerodromes were constructed at a rapid rate. In 1935 Coventry Corporation acquired land at Baginton for a municipal aerodrome and Birmingham City Council developed a municipal aerodrome at Elmdon, south-east of Birmingham. Private airfield landing grounds were also in use in Warwickshire: Leamington Spa (Maj. J.E. Bonniken); Woodley House, Kineton (Lord Willoughby de Broke); Milcote Hall, Stratford-upon-Avon (Mr J.A. Griffin); Lawford Heath (Mr D. Mitchell). These landing grounds were inspected by the Automobile Association and listed in the AA's *Register of Approved Landing Grounds*. A 1930s steel aircraft hangar survives at the former landing ground at Woodley House, Kineton.

Following Hitler's seizure of power in Germany in 1933, the threat from Nazi Germany resulted in a rearmament programme known as the Expansion Period. During the Expansion Period between 1934 and 1939, over eighty new RAF airfields were designed and built in Great Britain.

The airfield buildings of the Expansion Period were built to a high architectural standard in a well-proportioned neo-Georgian style. The architectural elevations were subject to approval by the Royal Fine Arts Commission and the positioning of buildings in relation to the countryside was subject to advice by the Society for the Preservation of Rural England. The airfield buildings were grouped in compact layouts to ease airfield operations, but with little regard for the effects of concentrated bombing.

At Coventry the Armstrong-Whitworth prototype Whitley bomber flew for the first time in March 1936. The Whitley was the first British all-metal heavy bomber. Production of the Whitley bomber moved from Whitley to a new factory at Baginton during 1936. Armstrong-Whitworth shared use of Baginton Airfield with Coventry City Corporation. Between 1936 and the termination of production in 1943, nearly 1,500 Whitleys were manufactured and on 19 March 1940 Whitleys dropped the first bombs to fall on Germany since 1918.

Within Warwickshire RAF Bramcote was one of the last Expansion Period airfields approved for construction prior to 1939.

Airfields 1939 to 1945: the Second World War

The Expansion Period airfield buildings were not economical in terms of materials used and speed of construction. When war broke out in 1939, work on incomplete Expansion Period airfields was accelerated by using prefabricated buildings and 'utility' construction methods.

From 1939 onwards, the design of new airfields adopted a policy of dispersed layout to reduce the effects of concentrated bombing. The technical site buildings and domestic site buildings were built in a dispersed layout.

By the end of the Second World War there were over 600 military airfields in Great Britain, including seventeen in Warwickshire.

Airfields 1946 to 2000: the Jet Age

Within two years of the end of the Second World War, ten out of the seventeen RAF airfields in Warwickshire were closed, and in most instances the land was returned to agricultural use.

Warwickshire has very close associations with the development of the jet engine. Frank Whittle was born in Coventry and was educated at Leamington College for Boys. From the late

1930s to the early 1940s, Whittle's headquarters for the design development of the jet engine was at Brownsover Hall near Rugby (the hall is now a hotel). Whittle's first prototype jet engine was tested on 12 April 1937 at the British Thomson-Houston factory, Rugby, and the maiden flight of the first British jet aircraft, the Gloster E28/39, took place at RAF Cranwell on 15 May 1941. Further test trials of the Gloster E28/39 were carried out at RAF Edgehill, Oxfordshire, close to the boundary with south Warwickshire. During July 1944 the first jet fighter to enter service with an RAF squadron was the twin-engine Gloster Meteor. Over 3,500 Meteors were manufactured, of which more than 1,000 were constructed at the Armstrong-Whitworth factory at Baginton. As a tribute to Sir Frank Whittle, a full-size fibreglass model of a Gloster E28/39 is displayed on the A4303 roundabout at Lutterworth.

(The Midland Air Museum at Baginton, incorporating the Sir Frank Whittle Jet Heritage Centre, is open all year round.)

As of April 1948, Vampire jet fighters were based at RAF Honiley, and in 1955 Sea Vampires from RAF Bramcote also began operations from the base.

During the early 1950s RAF Gaydon was completely reconstructed. In March 1954 it re-opened and became the first V-bomber base in Britain. RAF Gaydon's role as a V-bomber base is described in the Cold War section of this book. Following the closure in 1963 of RAF Wellesbourne Mountford, RAF Gaydon was the only operational RAF airfield in Warwickshire, right up until its own eventual closure in 1974.

Warwickshire Second World War RAF Airfields

During the Second World War there were seventeen active RAF military airfields and landing grounds in Warwickshire. The locations of Second World War airfields at Castle Bromwich, Elmdon and Hockley Heath are now, since the 1974 boundary re-drawings, within the West Midlands Metropolitan County.

SUMMARY OF WARWICKSHIRE RAF AIRFIELDS			
RAF MILITARY AIRFIELD	RAF BASE	MAIN ROLE DURING THE SECOND WORLD WAR AND CURRENT USE	RAF CLOSED
1. Bramcote	6/1940	Training base for instructors mainly using Oxfords, Tutors and Wellingtons. Transferred to Fleet Air Arm (December 1946) and became HMS *Gamecock*. Closed to flying in 1957 and site transferred to the Army in 1959. Now known as Gamecock Barracks. The M69 motorway follows the route of the former main runway. Pre-Second World War Expansion Period buildings survive, including C-Type hangars, barrack blocks, technical and domestic buildings. Second World War pillboxes survive in areas remote from the Gamecock Barracks.	11/1946

RAF MILITARY AIRFIELD	RAF BASE	MAIN ROLE DURING THE SECOND WORLD WAR AND CURRENT USE	RAF CLOSED
2. Ansty	1/1940	Training base for RAF pilots from 1940 to 1944. Also used as a base for assembly and testing the airspeed of Oxford and Mosquito aircraft manufactured by the Standard Motor Co. during the Second World War. Site now used by Rolls-Royce for the manufacture of industrial and marine gas turbine engines.	3/1953
3. Brinklow	10/1941	Satellite landing ground (SLG) used for the storage and repair of aircraft. Occasionally used by training aircraft from RAF Ansty and RAF Church Lawford. The land is now used for farming.	12/1945
4. Church Lawford	5/1941	Training base for instructors, mainly using Oxfords and Tutors. Land now used for farming and landfill, and the hangars are used for light industry and storage. Second World War buildings surviving include hangars, control tower, gymnasium, technical buildings and one pillbox.	1955
5. Baginton	9/1940	Used as a municipal airfield since 1930 with the help of nearby Armstrong-Whitworth Aircraft (AWA) who used the airfield for testing aircraft. AWA played an important part in the design and manufacture of British aircraft, particularly the Whitley and Lancaster bombers. A Midland air defence fighter group was based at Baginton during the Second World War. AWA closed in 1965. The airfield is still in use as Coventry Airport. The Midland Air Museum is located on the perimeter of the airfield. Four Second World War Bellman hangars survive.	1945
6. Honiley	5/1941	Main role was a night fighter station equipped with Beaufighters. After the Second World War Mosquitos were followed by Vampires. In 1955 RNVR Sea Vampires and Attackers were based at Honiley The land is now used for vehicle testing and farming.	3/1958

RAF MILITARY AIRFIELD	RAF BASE	MAIN ROLE DURING THE SECOND WORLD WAR AND CURRENT USE	RAF CLOSED
7. Warwick	12/1941	Located by A429 Stratford Road, south of Warwick. Relief Landing Ground (RLG) for Church Lawford. Land now used for farming and residential housing.	12/1945
8. Leamington Spa	12/1941	Located 3 miles south of Leamington Spa. Grass landing strip established in the late 1930s. Used for the repair of Hampden and Whitley bombers and also as a Relief Landing Ground (RLG) for Church Lawford and Ansty. Hangars now used for storage and light industry.	12/1945
9. Southam	6/1940	Relief Landing Ground (RLG) for Ansty and Church Lawford's Oxfords and Tutors. Land now used for farming.	12/1944
10. Snitterfield	3/1943	Flying Training School and satellite for Church Lawford. Designed for bombers but mainly used for training using Oxfords. The land is now used by a gliding club, a golf course and some for farming.	1946
11. Wellesbourne Mountford	4/1941	Main role was a Wellington bomber crew training station. Land now used by flying clubs, markets, light industry and Wellesbourne Wartime Museum. Various Second World War buildings survive including a J-type hangar and BHQ.	1963
12. Gaydon	6/1942	Main role during the Second World War was a Wellington bomber crew training station. Rebuilt during 1953 and re-opened as the first V-bomber crew training station equipped with Valiants in January 1955 and eventually Victors. Ceased as V-bomber station 1965. Site now used by Ford as a design and test centre for Land Rover and Jaguar and for the production of Aston Martin cars. The Heritage Motor Centre museum is also located on the site. Various buildings survive from the V-bomber station era including hangars, control tower and technical buildings.	10/1974

RAF MILITARY AIRFIELD	RAF BASE	MAIN ROLE DURING THE SECOND WORLD WAR AND CURRENT USE	RAF CLOSED
13. Stratford (Atherstone)	4/1941	Located 3.5 miles south of Stratford-upon-Avon, near Atherstone-on-Stour. Initially named RAF Atherstone, but changed due to another airfield known as Atherstone. Satellite for Wellesbourne Mountford and Pershore. Land now used for farming. Various Second World War buildings survive including a B1 hangar, control tower, BHQ, pillboxes, shooting range, bomb store and air-raid shelters.	11/1945
14. Long Marston	11/1941	Satellite for neighbouring RAF Honeybourne, flying Wellingtons, Hampdens and Whitleys. Land now used for various purposes, e.g. drag racing, flying clubs, markets and an aircraft museum. Various Second World War buildings survive, including remote dispersed technical and domestic buildings.	1954
15. Castle Bromwich	1926	Allocated to the Army Co-operation Command who trained anti-aircraft gun crews and searchlight crews. Adjacent to the airfield was a factory famous for producing over 11,500 Spitfires and also Lancaster bombers, which were test flown from the airfield. Land now used for commercial and residential housing.	4/1958
16. Elmdon	5/1939	Flying Training School and test flying of Hurricanes, Stirlings and Lancasters built by the Austin Motor Co. at the Longbridge works. Elmdon is now Birmingham International Airport.	2/1946
17. Hockley Heath	12/1941	Relief Landing Ground (RLG) for Elmdon and Church Lawford. Located to the north-west of Hockley Heath. Land now used for farming.	12/1945

In addition to the seventeen active RAF airfields, airfields were also considered, but not constructed, at the following locations:

| Astley | Proposed as an RLG for RAF Honiley |
| Copston Magna | Proposed as a medium bomber base |

Airfield Buildings and Structures

The following are summaries of the main categories of RAF airfield buildings and structures with examples in Warwickshire:

Runways

The majority of Second World War airfields had three runways, set as near to 60 degrees to each other as possible, to form the shape of an 'A' when viewed from above. The ends of the runways were connected by perimeter hard taxi tracks. Aircraft dispersal standings were constructed adjacent to the perimeter taxi tracks.

Before 1938 airfield runways were normally grassed, but with the development of heavy bombers it became necessary to provide hard runways constructed from tarmac or concrete. Alternative temporary runway hard surfaces were constructed by covering the grass with pierced steel planking, square grid track, bar and rod tracking or 'Sommerfeld Track'.

Warwickshire's Second World War RAF airfields at Ansty, Brinklow, Baginton, Hockley Heath, Leamington Spa, Southam and Warwick retained grass runways throughout the conflict and the remaining Warwickshire airfields had tarmac or concrete runways.

One exception was RAF Bramcote that was provided with three Sommerfeld Track runways. Sommerfeld Track consisted of woven wire chain-link mesh with metal rods threaded through it at 200mm intervals. The ends of the metal rods were looped to accept metal bars and enable the track to be joined up into a continuous surface. The runways at RAF Bramcote were under construction before the Air Ministry's decision to install permanent hard runways.

Hangars

Prior to the Expansion Period there were relatively few standard designs for permanent aircraft hangars. During the Expansion Period a variety of new designs were developed to accommodate larger aircraft. Examples are Types C, D, E, J, K, L and Lamella. The Type C was expensive to build and between 1934 and 1939 there were various design modifications to reduce costs. The 1938 version was known as Type C1 or Type C Protected Type. The Type C1 incorporated changes to the overall height, roof design and wall infilling using concrete or asbestos sheet cladding in lieu of brickwork. Five Type C1 hangars were constructed at RAF Bramcote. Two C1 hangars (AB01) survive and are used by the army within Gamecock Barracks.

Types D, E, L and Lamella hangars were curved-roof hangars, favoured for storage of reserve aircraft at Aircraft Storage Units (ASUs). The main differences between these types were in the size and type of construction.

Types D and E were of reinforced concrete construction, and the Type L and Lamella had lattice steel roof construction with various roof covering options. Types D, E, L and Lamella were not constructed at any of the Warwickshire RAF airfields.

Types J and K hangars were introduced during 1939 to reduce costs and speed-up the building programme. Type J and K hangars were all-steel constructions with curved-roof trusses, covered with mild steel plates and corrugated sheet-steel wall cladding. One Type J hangar (Type 5836/39) (AB02) exists at the former RAF base at Wellesbourne Mountford. The hangar is now utilised by light industry.

AB01 Type C1 hangar 3 at former RAF Bramcote, now Gamecock Barracks (September 2006).

Left: AB01 Type C1 hangar 4 at former RAF Bramcote, now Gamecock Barracks (September 2006).

Below: AB02 Type J hangar, at former RAF Wellesbourne Mountford (August 2006).

Right: AB03 Type T1 hangars, at former RAF Wellesbourne Mountford (August 2006).

Below: AB04 Bellman hangars (Type 8349/37) at former RAF Baginton (June 2006). (Courtesy of Air Atlantique Classic Flight)

In 1936 the Air Ministry issued specification requirements to various design companies for a low-cost transportable hangar that could be easily erected or dismantled. Designs from two companies, Bellman and Callender, were short-listed, and in 1938 the Bellman design was selected as the Air Ministry standard transportable hangar. Four 'Bellman' hangars (Type 8349/37) (AB04) survive at former RAF Baginton. Bellman hangars (AB05) also survive at former RAF Church Lawford and are used there for storage.

By 1940 the Bellman hangar design had become obsolete and various new designs for transportable hangars were developed. Examples designed and produced are Type T, Type S, Blister Types A and B, and Robins hangars. The Type T hangar was one of the most common types of hangar during the Second World War and a range of design types were manufactured. At former RAF Wellesbourne Mountford four Type T1 hangars (AB03) exist and at former RAF Baginton three Type T2 hangars (AB06) exist.

The Blister hangar was a simple arched hangar with steel sheeting roof. Each end of the hangar had canvas curtains or at some airfields one end was infilled with brickwork. Miskins & Sons constructed the prototype during 1940.

Left: AB06 Type T2 hangars at former RAF Baginton (June 2006). (Courtesy of Air Atlantique Classic Flight)

Below: AB06 Type T2 hangar interior at former RAF Baginton (June 2006). (Courtesy of Air Atlantique Classic Flight)

Three main types of Blister hangar were manufactured:

1. **Standard Blister** – Timber arched ribs at 5ft (1.5m) centres. 25ft long x 45ft span x 14ft high. (7.6m long x 13.7m span x 4.3m high).
2. **Over Blister** – Steel arched ribs at 7ft 6in (2.3m) centres. 45ft long x 65ft span x 19ft 10in high. (13.7m long x 19.8m span x 6m high).
3. **Extra Over Blister** – Steel arched ribs at 7ft 6in centres. 45ft long x 69ft span x 20ft 4in high. (13.7m long x 21m span x 6.2m high).

Blister hangars were erected at many of Warwickshire's Second World War airfields including Church Lawford (ten), Honiley (twelve), Warwick (four), Southam (six), Snitterfield (six), Wellesbourne Mountford (one), Elmdon (nine) and Hockley Heath (six). Unfortunately none of these hangars survive.

The Blister hangar provided at Wellesbourne Mountford was an Extra Over Blister and was fitted out with facilities for air-gunnery training.

The exposed steel framework of one Blister hangar at former RAF Warwick could be viewed from the Stratford Road, Warwick until 2003. The hangar frame was donated to the Felthorpe Flying Group who dismantled it and transported it to their headquarters near Norwich during September 2003.

The Ministry of Aircraft Production financed the design and production of the Type A and Type B prefabricated hangars. One Type B1 hangar (AB08) exists at the former RAF Stratford base and is currently used for industrial purposes.

Watch Offices or Control Towers

The watch office or control tower is the building from which the movement of aircraft is controlled. The name 'watch office' originated in the First World War era, while 'control tower' came into favour during the Second World War and originated from the USA. Before 1939 the buildings were generally single storey but during the six years of conflict two-storey control towers were provided and later extended with observation rooms added to the roof.

Within Warwickshire, control towers survive at the former RAF airfields at Bramcote, Church Lawford, Gaydon, Long Marston and Stratford. The control tower at Gaydon was constructed during 1953 and is described within the Cold War section of this book.

Above: AB09 Control tower (2328/39) at former RAF Bramcote; south elevation. (September 2006).

Right: AB09 Control tower (2328/39) at former RAF Bramcote; west elevation. (September 2006).

Above: AB10 Type B (7345/41) control tower at former RAF Long Marston (May 2006).

AB11 Control tower at former Stratford (June 2006).

AB12 Control tower at former RAF Church Lawford (June 2006).

The control tower (AB09) at former RAF Bramcote (now Gamecock Barracks) was built during the Expansion Period and included meteorological rooms. The design was Air Ministry drawing 2328/39 and is all concrete in construction. Gamecock Barracks army personnel currently use the building for sports changing rooms and recreational purposes.

One Type B (7345/41) control tower (AB10) with operations room and attached crew briefing room exists at Long Marston. The building was derelict for a number of years but is now refurbished and used by a light aircraft group while the surviving control tower (AB11) at former RAF Stratford has two stories and originally included operations and crew briefing rooms. The building is currently derelict.

The surviving type 12779/41 control tower (AB12) at former RAF Church Lawford is situated adjacent to a landfill site and sand and gravel extraction works. Also adjacent to the control tower are derelict operations buildings.

Technical and Administrative Buildings

Examples of technical and administrative buildings are workshops, photographic blocks, motor transport facilities, bulk fuel stores, engine test houses, station armouries, guardhouses, station headquarters, operations buildings, bomb-stores, water towers, parachute stores and general stores.

Within Warwickshire, many of the technical and administration buildings were of short-life utility construction, and many have been demolished. At the former RAF base in Bramcote (now Gamecock Barracks), a number of buildings survive from the Expansion Period including the entrance guardhouse (AB13), station headquarters (AB14), motor transport buildings (AB15), workshops (AB16) and administrative buildings (AB17).

AB13 Entrance guardhouse at former RAF Bramcote (September 2006).

AB14 Station headquarters at former RAF Bramcote (September 2006).

Above: AB18 Water tower, at former RAF Stratford (June 2006).

Left: AB19 Stores building, at former RAF Stratford (June 2006).

The lattice steelwork water tower (AB18) survives at former RAF Stratford but the water tank has been replaced with modern telecommunications equipment. At former RAF Stratford a storage shed (AB19) survives at the dispersed technical buildings site (AB20). A number of the technical buildings are currently used for office accommodation. Also surviving at former RAF Stratford is a bomb store (AB21) with reinforced concrete roof and brick walls.

A fire tender building (AB22) survives at former RAF Church Lawford and shooting ranges survive at former RAF Bramcote (AB23) and RAF Stratford (AB24).

Instructional Buildings

Examples of instructional buildings include various synthetic trainer buildings and classrooms that were used for training pilots, navigators, bomb-aimers, gunnery crews and mechanics. Many of Warwickshire's Second World War airfields were designated Operational Training Units (OTUs) and were thus provided with utility short-life instructional buildings. However, many of these buildings have since been demolished.

At former RAF Long Marston there is a surviving example of a Combined Turret Trainer and Air Ministry Laboratory (AML) Bombing Teacher building (AB25). The right-hand side of the building was single-storey and contained screen projector equipment and a turret simulator for training air gunners. The left-hand side of the building was two storeys high with a mezzanine platform. The top floor was a projection room from which a photographic aerial moving image of the ground was projected onto the ground floor. The mezzanine floor was fitted with bombsight and navigational equipment for training the bomb aimer and pilot. The trainee bomb aimer would lie in a prone position at the mezzanine floor level looking down through a bombsight at the moving image on the ground floor. When the bomb release button was pressed the moving ground image was stopped and the bomb drop location marked.

AB25 Turret trainer and bombing teacher at former RAF Long Marston (August 2006).

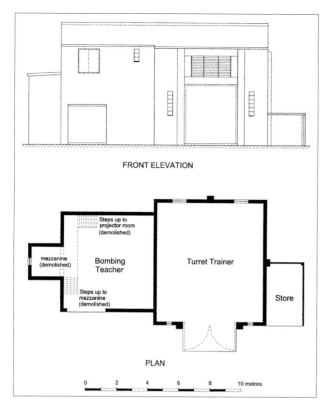

FRONT ELEVATION

Steps up to
projector room
(demolished)

mezzanine
(demolished)

**Bombing
Teacher**

Turret Trainer

Steps up to
mezzanine
(demolished)

Store

PLAN

0   2   4   6   8   10 metres

Left: AB25 Combined turret trainer and bombing teacher at former RAF Long Marston: plan and front elevation.

Below: AB27 Officers' mess at former RAF Bramcote (September 2006).

AB28 Type 8/84 H-block
barracks at former RAF
Bramcote (September
2006).

Domestic and Communal Buildings

Examples of domestic and communal buildings are barracks, mess quarters, NAAFI, dining
facilities, decontamination buildings, ablution blocks, sports facilities and station sick quarters.

Examples of Expansion Period barrack blocks, sergeants' messes (AB26) and officers' messes
(AB27) survive at former RAF Bramcote and are in army use (Gamecock Barracks). The type
8/84 H-block barracks (AB28) incorporated underground air-raid shelters each with emergency
escape tunnels to external ground-level hatches.

Utility build domestic and communal buildings (AB29) survive at former RAF Long Marston.
They were built in dispersed locations to the east of the airfield on the opposite side of the
B4632 road. The main dispersed sites were four living quarter sites, a communal site and a WAAF
communal and living quarter site. The main surviving buildings at the communal site consisted
of dining facilities, stores, messes, bathhouses, ablutions, sick quarters, a decontamination centre,
offices and other ancillary facilities. RAF personnel used the buildings during the Second
World War, but after 1945 the buildings were used for army and refugee accommodation. Polish
refugees occupied the buildings until the early 1980s, during which period various modifications
were carried out to the accommodation.

At former RAF Stratford domestic and communal buildings (AB30) survive in dispersed
locations, while RAF gymnasium buildings survive at former RAF Church Lawford (AB31)
and RAF Gaydon (AB32). RAF officers' and airmen's married quarters housing exists at former
RAF Bramcote, Church Lawford, Baginton, Honiley, Wellesbourne Mountford and Gaydon.
With the exception of Bramcote the houses are privately owned and occupied.

At former RAF Stratford a derelict gas decontamination building (AB33) survives. The
building was designed to treat victims of gas attacks, while the primary rooms within the
decontamination building were undressing areas, air lock lobbies, first aid areas, decontamination
showers, dressing rooms, stores, boiler room, ventilation plant room and a roof-mounted water
tank room. With reference to the picture of AB33 (page 51), in the front elevation are two
entrances, one for wounded victims and one for unwounded victims. The two horizontal slots

in the wall were for the disposal of contaminated clothing into storage bins. To the rear of the building is a tall brick shaft designed to intake air from above the poisonous gas zone. A mechanical ventilation system maintained a positive air pressure within the building to prevent the ingress of poisonous gases. The air was exhausted from the building via wall-mounted cowls. The partially visible structure on the roof is the water tank room.

Left and below: AB29 Domestic and communal buildings at former RAF Long Marston (June 2006).

AB33 Gas
decontamination
building at former
RAF Stratford
(August 2006).

Prefabricated Huts

Prefabricated huts were used extensively at the majority of airfields constructed during the Second World War. The wide variety of types and materials used was influenced by the supply availability of materials under wartime conditions. Examples of prefabricated hut types include:

1. **Nissen huts** – Semicircular in section and basically of curved corrugated steel sheet roofs supported by 'T' section steel ribs. The end sections were infilled with timber boarding or brick walls.
2. **Timber Huts** – Prefabricated timber frame sectional walls with external weatherboarding and lined internally with plasterboard. Roof construction was of timber trusses with timber boards and felt or corrugated asbestos sheeting.
3. **British Concrete Federation (BCF) huts** – Walls consisted of inner and outer standard prefabricated concrete panels fitted between concrete vertical posts at 0.99m (3ft 3in) centres. Roof construction was of lightweight concrete breeze slabs covered with felt or corrugated asbestos sheeting.
4. **Orlit huts** – Walls consisted of inner and outer standard prefabricated concrete planks fitted between reinforced concrete I-section vertical posts at 1.8m (6ft) centres. Roof construction was of concrete slabs covered in felt. Orlit huts were more economical than BCF huts because the vertical posts were spaced at wider centres.
5. **Ministry of Works (MoW) standard huts** – These were designed as a cheaper alternative to BCF and Orlit huts. They basically consisted of prefabricated, reinforced concrete transverse frames with different wall infill options e.g. concrete, brick, timber boards, felted plasterboard or wood cement. Roofs were generally corrugated asbestos.
6. **Romney huts** – These buildings were semicircular in section and consisted of curved corrugated steel sheet roofs supported by 65mm (2.5in) steel tube curved ribs. The ends were generally infilled with flat corrugated steel sheeting. The internal span was 10.7m (35ft) and the length was in multiples of 2.4m (8ft). Romney stores were generally used as stores or workshops.

AB35 Nissen hut at former RAF Long Marston (June 2006).

Within Warwickshire examples of Nissen huts survive at former RAF Baginton (AB34) and RAF Long Marston (AB35). One Romney hut (AB36) survives at former RAF Long Marston at the dispersed communal site.

Bombing Ranges

For the training of Second World War bomber aircrew, target area bombing ranges were provided. Within Warwickshire the following were designated bombing ranges:

Grandborough	Bombing for Operational Training Unit (OTU)
Priors Hardwick	Bombing for 28 Operational Training Unit (28 OTU)
Shotteswell	Bombing for 12 Operational Training Unit (12 OTU)
Idlicote	Bombing for 24 Operational Training Unit (24 OTU)

The bombing ranges were open fields near the four villages mentioned above. Overlooking the target area at each range were quadrant observation towers. The observers in the towers took bearings of each practice bomb drop and radioed the results to the training aircraft.

AB36 Romney hut at former RAF Long Marston (August 2006).

The towers near Grandborough and Priors Hardwick have in recent years been demolished. The villagers of Shotteswell are reported to have suffered more from the RAF than they ever did from the Luftwaffe!

For training, non-explosive practice bombs were generally used. Early in the war the typical weight of a practice bomb was 11kg (25lb) and as the war progressed the size and weight of bombs increased. The M38 practice bomb weighing 45kg (100lb) was filled with sand and a charge of black powder to indicate the impact location.

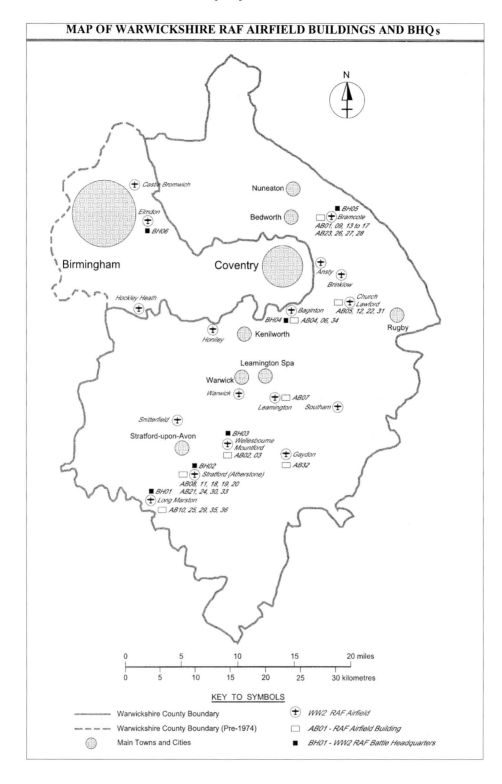

MAP OF WARWICKSHIRE RAF AIRFIELD BUILDINGS AND BHQs

N

Castle Bromwich
Nuneaton

■ *BH05*
Elmdon
□ ✛ *Bramcote*
Bedworth
AB01, 09, 13 to 17
■ *BH06*
AB23, 26, 27, 28

Birmingham
Coventry
✛ *Ansty*
✛ *Brinklow*

Hockley Heath
Church
□ ✛ *Lawford*
AB05, 12, 22, 31
✛ *Baginton*
BH04 ■ □ *AB04, 06, 34*
Honiley
Kenilworth
Rugby

Leamington Spa
Warwick
Warwick ✛
✛ □ *AB07*
Leamington Southam ✛

Snitterfield ✛
Stratford-upon-Avon
■ *BH03*
✛ *Wellesbourne Mountford*
□ *AB02, 03*
✛ *Gaydon*
■ *BH02*
□ *AB32*
□ ✛ *Stratford (Atherstone)*
AB08, 11, 18, 19, 20
■ *BH01* *AB21, 24, 30, 33*
✛ *Long Marston*
□ *AB10, 25, 29, 35, 36*

| 0 | 5 | 10 | 15 | 20 miles |
| 0 | 5 | 10 | 15 | 20 | 25 | 30 kilometres |

KEY TO SYMBOLS

— Warwickshire County Boundary
- - - Warwickshire County Boundary (Pre-1974)
⬤ Main Towns and Cities

✛ *WW2 RAF Airfield*
□ *AB01 - RAF Airfield Building*
■ *BH01 - WW2 RAF Battle Headquarters*

4

RAF Airfield Defences

Introduction

The defence of RAF airfields was subject to various changes of policy between 1934 and 1945. During the Expansion Period not a great deal of attention was given to airfield defences. Airfield facilities were generally grouped in compact layouts with defences close to the buildings.

From 1939 onwards the policy to disperse buildings and aircraft led to the installation of additional airfield perimeter defences. With the defeat of France in 1940 and the increased threat of invasion, further attention was given to airfield defences.

The Taylor Report, issued in September 1940, provided classifications for airfield defences based upon the location of the airfield and potential scale of attack:

Class 1:   Airfields within 20 miles of selected seaports
Class 2a: Airfields designated to provide aircraft to repel a potential invasion
Class 2b: Airfields within 5 miles of vulnerable points inland
Class 2c: Airfields utilised as Aircraft Storage Units (ASU)
Class 3:   Airfields not included in class 1 or 2 and considered a lower risk

The strength of the garrison and number of defences reduced in proportion from class 1 down to class 3.

Summary of Taylor Report Recommended Airfield Defence Works			
Defence Item	Class 1 Airfield	Class 2 Airfield	Class 3 Airfield
Pillboxes for inward defence	8–14	6–10	Combined total 10–16
Pillboxes for outward defence	12–18	9–14	
Pickett-Hamilton Forts	3	–	–
Dummy pillboxes	10–12	8	6

Defence Item	Class 1 Airfield	Class 2 Airfield	Class 3 Airfield
Rifle pits	As required	As required	As required
Armoured vehicles	4	3	1
Perimeter wire (around station buildings)	Total	Total	–
Local wire for defences posts	Total	Total	Total
Anti-aircraft defence posts	8	8	8

Following the German deployment of airborne troops to capture airfields in Crete during May 1941, the concept of perimeter defences was reviewed and the policy changed to the provision of strong points or 'defended localities' to defend airfield approaches and the open areas of the airfield. The emphasis of airfield defence was on preventing a successful enemy landing on the airfield and so defences generally faced both inwards and outwards. Mobility was also provided by trucks and armoured vehicles to quickly move defenders to trouble spots.

In February 1942 the RAF Regiment was created to defend RAF airfields, whereas prior to 1942 RAF personnel, Royal Artillery gunners and Army units had defended airfields.

Within Warwickshire the only Class 2a airfield was RAF Bramcote, with Class 2b airfields at RAF Baginton (Coventry), Castle Bromwich, Church Lawford and Elmdon (Birmingham). The remaining Warwickshire Second World War airfields were rated Class 3. Whilst these airfields were not as strategically important they were provided with various different types of defences. The number and extent of defences varied, with the degree of defence partly depending on the importance of the airfield. Examples of Second World War airfield defence structures include slit trenches, seagull trenches, barbed wire installations, gun emplacements, anti-aircraft guns, pillboxes, battle headquarters and passive defences.

Slit trenches for infantry firing positions were simple hand-dug trenches that were sometimes lined with timber or brickwork.

Seagull trenches consisted of trenches with a plan view resembling a letter 'W'. The trenches were protected by a flat concrete roof supported by columns to provide horizontal openings for fields of fire. The roof would normally have been covered with earth for additional protection and to provide camouflage. There are no known surviving seagull trenches in Warwickshire.

Examples of barbed wire installations include perimeter barbed wire fences, Dannert concertina wire obstacles and picket fences. Dannert concertina wire obstacles consisted of multiple coils of barbed wire installed in concertina rolls secured to steel vertical stakes. Triple Dannert wire consisted of three coils – two at the base and one positioned on top – while picket fences consisted of waist-high horizontal lines of barbed wire secured to steel or timber stakes.

Gun emplacements and anti-aircraft (AA) gun defences were often located in simple sandbagged or earthwork pits. Initially only light AA machine guns were available, such as Lewis guns, but as the war progressed the firepower was increased with the installation of medium AA and Bofors guns.

Airfield pillboxes were generally more substantial and carefully located compared with those built in 1940. The Air Ministry provided standard pillbox designs and the positioning of the pillboxes was carefully designed to integrate closely with the overall airfield defences. 'Turnbull' mounts, pivoting steel frames to support light machine guns, were fitted at the embrasures in many RAF airfield pillboxes.

The battle headquarters was a building from which the defence of the airfield would have been coordinated.

Examples of passive defences employed on Second World War airfields are dispersal areas for aircraft, protection of buildings with sand bags, air-raid shelters, taped windows, gas decontamination facilities and camouflage. Camouflage methods, such as painting buildings, painting hedge lines on runways, coloured rubber granules or wood chippings on runways and decoy sites to deceive the enemy to drop bombs away from the intended target, were also developed around this time.

With the closure of many RAF airfields at the end of the Second World War, many of the defences were demolished, trenches were filled and the land returned to agricultural use. However, a number of airfield pillboxes and battle headquarters have survived in Warwickshire, mainly due to the strength of reinforced concrete and their relative isolation from redevelopment areas.

Warwickshire RAF Airfield Pillboxes

The main types of pillboxes constructed at RAF airfields in Warwickshire were Type 22, Type 24, mushroom type and rectangular RAF variant type. Refer to Appendix 1 Warwickshire Pillbox Types for a summary and comparison of the pillbox types.

Other types of specialist pillboxes deployed nationally, mainly at airfields, were the Tett Turret, Allan-Williams Turret and the Pickett-Hamilton Fort. The Tett Turret was a two-man concrete cylindrical pillbox sunk into the ground complete with a revolving concrete turret. The Allan-Williams Turret consisted of a revolving steel turret positioned above a cylindrical pit. There are no known surviving Tett Turret or Allan-Williams Turret pillboxes in Warwickshire.

The Pickett-Hamilton Fort (RAF Type 13313/40), or 'disappearing pillbox', consisted of two large-diameter reinforced concrete pipes with one pipe sliding inside the other pipe. The pillbox was sunk into the ground and had an internal raising mechanism. During normal airfield operations the roof of the inner pipe would be flush with the ground surface, and in the event of an attack the inner pipe would be raised to provide defensive fire via rectangular loopholes. Due to various problems the construction of Pickett-Hamilton Forts was discontinued in March 1942. Warwickshire records indicate that several Pickett-Hamilton Forts were installed at RAF Lawford Heath, but it is unlikely that any have survived following redevelopment of the airfield.

The following are examples of RAF airfield pillboxes in Warwickshire:

PB31, PB32 and PB33 Mushroom pillboxes at former RAF Long Marston (NGR: SP 175494, SP 176494 and SP 175493)

Three 'mushroom' pillboxes located on rising ground to the north-east of the Long Marston Airfield runway and adjacent to battle headquarters BH01. The pillboxes would have provided a localised stronghold and defensive protection of the adjacent battle headquarters. Mushroom pillboxes (RAF Type 303/41) are also known as Cantilever Type or F.C. Construction Type. Each pillbox is partially below ground and has an internal diameter of 4260mm and 720mm-thick walls constructed of brickwork shuttering with concrete infill and concrete coping forming a complete ring. The circular roof construction is reinforced concrete supported by cruciform brickwork walls. The embrasure is 230mm high with a 360-degree continuous unrestricted view and uninterrupted field of fire. Each pillbox has two entrances positioned diagonally opposite with access via sunken holes lined with brickwork. The entrance sunken holes are partially filled in. A continuous steel tubular rail below the embrasure, for a light machine-gun mount, exists in each pillbox. Communication trenches may have linked the three pillboxes and adjacent battle headquarters.

PB33 Mushroom pillbox at former RAF Long Marston, with PB31 and PB32 in the background (June 2003).

PB34 and PB35 Pillboxes at former RAF Long Marston (NGR: SP 170496 and SP 170488)
Two destroyed pillboxes. Type not known.

PB36 and PB37 Type 24 pillboxes at former RAF Stratford (NGR: SP 219513 and SP 212520)
Two pillboxes located on private farmland. PB36 is located south of Ailstone Farm and PB37 is to the north of the former airfield perimeter track, adjacent to battle headquarters BH02. The pillboxes are standard type 24 irregular hexagon designs. Both are partially below ground with a ramp leading down to the entrance. Within the ramp wall are two storage recesses. The entrance face has two rifle embrasures and the other five wall faces each have one embrasure. The construction is reinforced concrete throughout with 380mm-thick walls, 300mm-thick roof and, internally, a 225mm-thick T-shaped blast/anti-ricochet wall. Within both pillboxes are loose concrete panels that would have been used for internally covering the embrasures. Fitted to one embrasure in PB37 is a 'Turnbull' steel pivoting machine-gun mount.

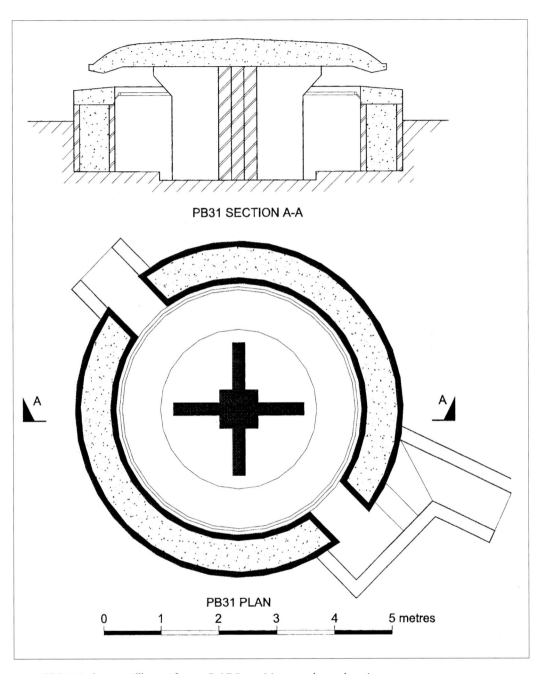

PB31 Mushroom pillbox at former RAF Long Marston: plan and section.

PB36 Type 24 pillbox at former RAF Stratford (June 2006).

PB37 Type 24 pillbox at former RAF Stratford (June 2006).

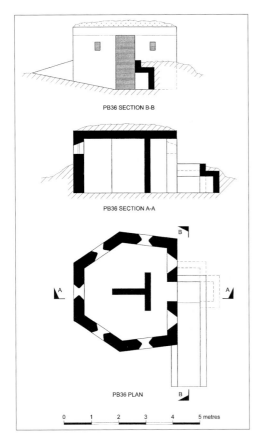

Above: PB37 Type 24 pillbox Turnbull machine-gun mount (June 2006).

Left: PB36 and PB37 Type 24 pillboxes at former RAF Stratford: plan and sections.

Below: PB38 Type 22 (variant) pillbox at former RAF Church Lawford (July 2003).

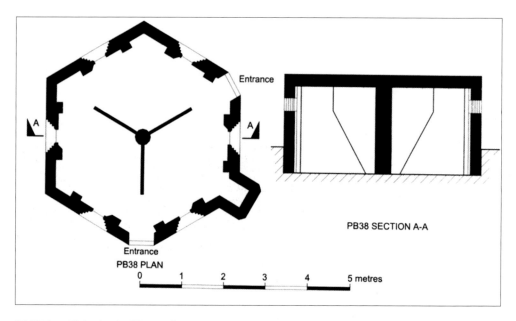

PB38 Type 22 (variant) pillbox at former RAF Church Lawford: plan and section.

PB38 Type 22 (variant) pillbox at former RAF Church Lawford (NGR: SP 454729)

This example is located on a public road verge near the original entrance to the former RAF Church Lawford Airfield. The pillbox is of reinforced concrete construction and hexagonal plan, with one embrasure located centrally in each of the six walls. Two entrances are positioned at the apex of the walls. One rectangular wall protrusion is located at a wall apex, forming a 460mm-wide x 560mm-deep, full height compartment inside the pillbox. Three angled concrete panel anti-ricochet walls radiate from a central concrete circular column. Five embrasures and one entrance are infilled with brickwork.

PB39 Type 24 pillbox at former RAF Church Lawford (NGR: SP 455735)

This pillbox was located near the former entrance to the airfield and has been destroyed.

PB40 RAF variant pillbox at former RAF Bramcote (NGR: SP 417876)

RAF Bramcote was provided with numerous pillboxes around the perimeter of the airfield and adjacent to the hangars. The pillboxes were rectangular non-standard local design. Gun pits for LAA guns were originally adjacent to many of the pillboxes. Many of the pillboxes have been destroyed following closure of the airfield and the later construction of the M69 motorway.

PB40 is located in a field adjacent to a minor road on high ground covering the south-east approaches to the former airfield. This is a rectangular pillbox with embrasures in each wall and each corner. The entrance is below one corner embrasure. The construction is of solid brickwork walls (350mm thick) with a reinforced concrete roof. Its condition is fair, with only some damage to the entrance. All embrasures are infilled with brickwork and the pillbox may have been used for an alternative purpose after initial construction.

PB40 RAF variant pillbox at former RAF Bramcote (July 2003).

PB41 RAF variant pillbox at former RAF Bramcote (July 2003).

PB41 RAF variant pillbox at former RAF Bramcote (NGR: SP 418875)

This particular pillbox is located in a field by the corner of the B4109 road and minor road to Bramcote. It is a rectangular pillbox with embrasures in the middle of each wall and each corner. The entrance is via a sunken hole below one corner embrasure. Construction is of solid brickwork walls (350mm thick) and a reinforced concrete roof. In the centre of the pillbox is a square brickwork support column. PB38 and PB40 do not have centre columns. Its condition is fair but the entrance is blocked with concrete and brickwork. All embrasures are open.

PB42 RAF variant pillbox at former RAF Bramcote (NGR: SP 405869)

This example is located on the verge of the B4109, near the entrance to Bramcote Mains. It is a rectangular pillbox with embrasures in each sidewall and each corner. The entrance is below one corner embrasure protected by a brickwork wall. Construction is of solid brickwork walls (350mm thick) with a reinforced concrete roof. All embrasures are open. The roof is currently utilised to support signage.

PB43 to PB57 Pillboxes at former RAF Bramcote

All fifteen RAF variant pillboxes at these locations were destroyed.

PB58 Pillbox at former RAF Bramcote (NGR: SP 405874)

This RAF variant pillbox is located within a private caravan storage compound. No public access is allowed for the reasons already outlined.

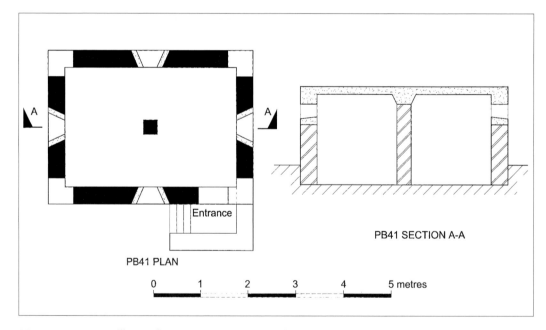

PB41 RAF variant pillbox at former RAF Bramcote: plan and section.

PB42 RAF variant pillbox at former RAF Bramcote (July 2003).

PB59 and PB60 Pillboxes at former RAF Baginton (NGR: SP 348746 and 349747)

These two pillboxes were originally located on the north-western perimeter of the airfield. Both have been destroyed.

PB61 Type 24 Pillbox at former RAF Elmdon (NGR: SP 163838)

One concrete type 24 pillbox was originally located on the western perimeter of the airfield north of the A45 road. The pillbox was destroyed during construction works sometime in the last decade.

Warwickshire RAF Airfield Battle Headquarters

In the event of an attack, primarily by airborne forces, the defence of the airfield would have been coordinated from the battle headquarters. The most common design was Air Ministry drawing No.11008/41. This design consisted of five underground rooms and a command observation post at one end with a clear 360-degree view through a horizontal slit protected by a reinforced concrete cupola. The main entrance was via a flight of concrete steps at the opposite end to the cupola. An emergency exit hatch was located adjacent to the cupola.

A less common design was the type 3329/41 which was smaller and had only one entrance via a manhole hatch. Warwickshire battle headquarters references BH01 and BH02 could possibly be type 3329/41; further research is necessary to verify the type.

BH01 RAF battle headquarters at former RAF Long Marston, with pillboxes PB31 and PB32 in the background (June 2003).

BH02 RAF battle headquarters at former RAF Stratford, with pillbox PB37 in the background (June 2006).

The following are examples of RAF military airfield battle headquarters in Warwickshire:

BH01 RAF battle headquarters at former RAF Long Marston (NGR: SP 175494)

This headquarters building is located on private land to the north-east of the Long Marston Airfield runway adjacent to three mushroom pillboxes. The only visible remains are the command observation post cupola and escape hatch. The escape hatch pit is partially filled with rubbish and water while the condition of the concrete cupola is good.

BH02 RAF battle headquarters at former RAF Stratford (NGR: SP 211 520)

Located on private farmland to the north of the former airfield perimeter track, this RAF installation was sited adjacent to pillbox PB37. The main entrance is filled in and the only visible remains are the command observation post cupola and escape hatch.

BH03 RAF battle headquarters at former RAF Wellesbourne Mountford (NGR: SP 265545)

Type 11008/41 BHQ is located inside the perimeter of the airfield adjacent to the Charlecote to Loxley road. The airfield is currently in use for private light aircraft. This battle headquarters has been renovated and is part of the Wellesbourne Wartime Museum, which has many interesting Second World War aviation exhibits. The museum is operated by volunteers and is normally open to the public on Sundays. The condition of this particular BHQ is good but occasionally suffers from flooding.

BH04 RAF battle headquarters at former RAF Baginton (NGR: SP 344741)

Type 11008/41 BHQ is located on private farmland not far from the current perimeter of Coventry airport. The headquarters was constructed on elevated ground overlooking the airfield and the river Sowe and is in a good condition with undamaged external guard rails to the entrance steps. The interior is not flooded due to its elevated location and well-drained surrounding land. The command observation cupola has one gun embrasure facing the airfield. This is an unusual feature for a battle headquarters because there is normally no provision for defensive fire.

BH03 RAF battle headquarters at former RAF Wellesbourne Mountford, with Vampire T11XK590 in the background (April 2003).

A general view of BH04 RAF battle headquarters at former RAF Baginton (August 2003).

BH04 RAF battle headquarters at former RAF Baginton – cupola embrasure (August 2003).

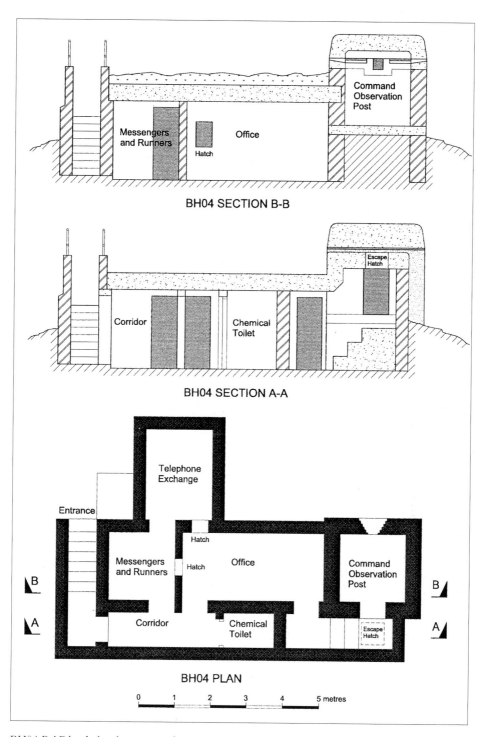

BH04 SECTION B-B

BH04 SECTION A-A

BH04 PLAN

0   1   2   3   4   5 metres

BH04 RAF battle headquarters at former RAF Baginton: plan and sections.

BH05 RAF battle headquarters at former RAF Elmdon (June 2006).

BH05 RAF battle headquarters at former RAF Bramcote (NGR: SP 415872)
This example of an RAF BHQ was demolished, probably during construction of the M69 motorway that crosses the former airfield.

BH06 RAF battle headquarters at former RAF Elmdon (NGR: SP 164836)
Type 11008/41 BHQ located immediately adjacent to the A45 Coventry Road on the opposite side to Birmingham International Airport, West Midlands. Prior to 1974 this BHQ was located within Warwickshire. Bushes and trees conceal the BHQ. The main entrance is partially blocked with rubbish while the escape hatch is missing but the steel cat ladder remains.

5

Warwickshire
Anti-Aircraft Sites

Introduction

During the First World War aircraft squadrons based at Castle Bromwich provided anti-aircraft defence for Warwickshire. Initially, anti-aircraft guns were merely adapted field guns, the first purpose-made anti-aircraft gun was a 3in calibre gun with an effective ceiling of 23500ft (1763m). During the First World War two 3in AA gun installations were located in the Coventry area at Wyken House and Radford, while twelve AA gun installations were located in Birmingham; these were equipped with 3in and 18-pounder guns. Prior to the Second World War ground-based anti-aircraft defences were improved, and this section describes Second World War anti-aircraft defences in Warwickshire and provides a short overview of the Coventry Blitz. With the onset of the Cold War, Britain's anti-aircraft radar defences were upgraded and this is also briefly described in the Cold War radar and telecommunications section.

The following types of anti-aircraft defences were deployed in Warwickshire during the Second World War:

> Heavy anti-aircraft artillery (HAA)
> Light anti-aircraft artillery (LAA)
> Searchlights
> Barrage balloons
> Bombing decoys sites (refer to the next section of this book)

Heavy Anti-Aircraft Artillery (HAA)

Coventry and Birmingham were classified as Gun Defended Areas (GDAs) and so were provided with HAA batteries. Prior to 1942 Coventry had ten designated HAA battery sites (site codes A to L), while Birmingham had twenty-one (site codes A to U). However, by 1942 Coventry and Birmingham GDAs had been amalgamated and the HAA batteries were renumbered using a sequence of site codes from H1 to H72. The number of batteries and guns deployed fluctuated throughout the Second World War and in some instances designated battery sites were not even armed. It was not unusual for artillery to be moved from site to site.

The purpose of HAA was to engage high-altitude enemy aircraft. The three main HAA gun types deployed in the Coventry and Birmingham GDAs at the start of hostilities in 1939 were the 3in calibre, 3.7in calibre and the 4.5in calibre. The following is a snapshot example of the approximate number of guns deployed in December 1940:

HAA GUNS DEPLOYED (DECEMBER 1940)		
Gun Calibre	Coventry GDA	Birmingham GDA
4.5in	0	16
3.7in (static)	16	32
3.7in (mobile)	16	47
3in	8	0
Total	40	95

The 4.5in calibre gun had an effective ceiling of 34500ft (10516m). The 3.7in calibre gun, Marks 1 to 3, each had an effective ceiling of 32000ft (9754m). Mobile and static versions of the 3.7in gun were manufactured throughout the war and improved types were developed through to the Mark 6 that had an effective ceiling of 45000ft (13716m).

Within the Coventry GDA the main 3.7in gun HAA batteries consisted of four guns in individual gun pits with a separate command post building and other associated facilities. The gun pits were normally circular with the gun located in the centre and secured to a concrete base with holdfast bolts. Surrounding the circular concrete base were ammunition lockers and one or two shelters for the gun crew.

The lockers and shelters were constructed from light concrete blocks and provided with reinforced concrete roofs. Earth banks around the perimeter of the gun pit blockwork walls provided blast protection from enemy bombs.

The command post building was usually a partially underground structure with banked earth blast protection against concrete block walls and a reinforced concrete roof. Open enclosures within the structure were designed to contain height or range-finder equipment, a spotter's telescope or binoculars, a predictor (mechanical computer) and, at some sites, a light anti-aircraft gun. Rooms within the command post building included a plotting room, telephone/communications room, staff rest room and machinery rooms.

The approach of enemy aircraft was detected by remote radar and visual observation by the Royal Observer Corps (ROC). Information on the height and direction of the aircraft was telephoned to the appropriate HAA battery's command post. The command post height finder crew would measure the height of the aircraft and pass this on to the predictor crew. The predictor would calculate the bearing, elevation and correct fuse setting for the shells to explode at the correct height. This information was automatically transmitted via cables to the dials of the HAA guns. The 3.7in guns were each operated by a crew of nine.

At night during the first year of the war, the location of aircraft was detected using acoustic sound locator equipment. However, the sound locators proved to be ineffective, and from 1940 onwards were replaced with gun-laying radar that progressively improved in performance throughout the war.

Right and below: 3.7in heavy anti-aircraft guns at Fort Paull near Kingston upon Hull. Both the mobile and static versions were deployed in Warwickshire. (Photographs courtesy of Mike Osborne)

Other facilities associated with HAA batteries were buildings for magazines, guardhouses, personnel accommodation huts, officers' quarters, stores, workshops and sewage plants.

Light Anti-Aircraft Artillery (LAA)

The primary purpose of LAA guns was to engage low-flying enemy aircraft. Many different types of LAA guns were used during the Second World War, including Lewis guns, Bren guns, 20mm Oerliken guns, two pounder pom-pom guns and 40mm Bofors guns. The larger calibre LAA guns were manufactured in both mobile and static versions.

LAA guns were deployed in Warwickshire to protect towns, factories and railways. The gun emplacements were generally insubstantial, comprising little more than circular earthworks, sandbags and occasionally earth-protected blockwork walls. Portable ammunition lockers would have been provided and at some sites there was a basic shelter for the gun crew, within Warwickshire there are few obvious remains of these installations; many are only visible as crop circles on aerial photographs.

40mm Bofors light anti-aircraft gun at Coalhouse Fort, East Tilbury, Essex. The Bofors gun was deployed at various Warwickshire LAA sites.

Searchlights

Searchlight installations were located throughout the country. Prior to the development of radar the operation of searchlights was the only method of identifying aircraft targets at night. Searchlights also discouraged aircraft from flying low and thus had the effect of reducing bombing accuracy. During the early years of the Second World War, in conjunction with searchlights, sound locator units were used to identify where the aircraft noise was greatest and so enable the searchlights to be more accurately pointed. With the development of radar and increased aircraft speeds, sound locator units were phased out.

Searchlight installations generally consisted of a circular earthwork for the searchlight, light anti-aircraft gun pits, crew accommodation huts, sound locator unit, predictor unit and a generator. Within Warwickshire there is a dearth of searchlight installation remains and many can now only be seen as crop circles on aerial photographs.

Barrage Balloons

Barrage balloons were installed at vulnerable sites to force enemy aircraft to fly high, which would hopefully have the dual effect of reducing bombing accuracy and providing an easier target for anti-aircraft guns and fighter aircraft. Numerous barrage balloons were installed around Birmingham and Coventry. A German Junkers 88A bomber crashed at Witheybrook, Coventry, on 16 September 1940 after hitting a barrage balloon. Unfortunately, allied aircraft also collided with barrage balloons; a Hampden bomber crashed after hitting one at Coventry on 24 May 1940. Balloons were tethered to 5-ton lorries or concrete blocks embedded in the ground. There are no known surviving remains of barrage balloon installations in Warwickshire.

The Coventry Blitz – Moonlight Sonata

There are many articles and book references regarding the devastating bombing of Coventry on the night of 14 November 1940, which caused over 500 fatalities, over 400 serious injuries, and left many buildings destroyed. There has been much controversy as to whether British intelligence knew of the proposed attack well in advance of it occurring. Current available evidence indicates that on 11 November 1940, the Bletchley Park Ultra team decrypted a German message which indicated that the German operation code 'Moonlight Sonata' was to be a forthcoming major bombing operation. However, the decrypted message did not indicate the date and location of the operation target.

To counter the Moonlight Sonata operation the RAF set up a plan known as Cold Water that would commence once the Moonlight Sonata operation commenced. The Luftwaffe used several different types of radar navigational systems such as Knickebein, X-Apparatus and Y-Apparatus. These systems basically used intersecting radar beams and timing devices to guide bombers to their targets. During mid-afternoon on 14 November, British radar listening stations detected X-Apparatus beams that aligned on Coventry. The Cold Water counter plan was put into action. The main elements of Cold Water are listed below and the outcome is given in brackets:

1. Continuous monitoring of German radio signals and jamming of navigational beams. (The German X-Apparatus system was a relatively new system and the British jamming apparatus was set at an incorrect frequency to jam the German beam system.)
2. RAF bombing raids over German bomber fields in France, Belgium and Holland with heavy raids on the Moonlight Sonata airfields in France. (Ineffective.)
3. RAF bombing attack on the Cherbourg beam transmitters. (Ineffective.)
4. RAF bombing raid on Berlin. (Ineffective.)
5. Deploy the maximum number of night fighters possible. (Over 100 were deployed, but only one bomber was damaged by a night fighter.)
6. Deploy additional AA guns. (The target was confirmed too late to send additional AA guns. During the raid only two bombers were brought down by AA fire.)

The night of 14 November was bright and moonlit with clear skies and it is generally recorded that the German bomber force would have found the target with little difficulty after the leading bombers had dropped their incendiary bombs. Unfortunately, the raid demonstrated the ineffectiveness of night air defences during the early years of the Second World War.

From 1941 onwards the British air defences were continuously upgraded by improvements to gun-laying radar, night fighter radar, searchlight radar, bombing decoys, gun-defended areas, proximity shells and changes to tactics. During late 1941 the night interception tactics system code named Smack was deployed. This basically involved the repositioning of searchlights to form Indicator and Killer zones for the night fighters. This, in conjunction with night fighter radio control, increased night fighter interceptions of bombers. The industrial areas of the Midlands were designated as gun defended areas and the Indicator and Killer zones were established around the gun defended areas.

Warwickshire Anti-Aircraft Installations

The following are examples of Warwickshire's Second World War anti-aircraft installation sites:

AA01, AA02 and AA03 Searchlight batteries

Three searchlight battery sites were located near Butlers Marston, Wellesbourne and Bishop's Tachbrook. They were identified as circular crop marks on aerial photographs. See Appendix 2 for grid locations.

AA04 and A05 Anti-aircraft batteries

Two light anti-aircraft batteries were located near Radford Semele and Copt Green, close to Lapworth. They too were identified as circular crop marks on aerial photographs. See Appendix 2 for grid locations.

AA06 Nuthurst HAA battery near Hockley Heath (NGR: SP130719)

A heavy anti-aircraft battery was located 1 mile west of Nuthurst, near Hockley Heath. The installation of the guns did not take place and the site buildings have since been demolished. The Site code was H11 within the Birmingham Gun Defended Area (GDA).

AA07 Bannerhill HAA battery near Kenilworth (NGR: SP 275693)

Four-gun heavy anti-aircraft battery located on private farmland adjacent to a private farm road and public footpath, near Goodrest Farm, 100m south of Rouncil Lane, Kenilworth.

This installation had the site code H25 within the Coventry Gun Defended Area (GDA). The battery consists of four gun pits and a command post building. During the war each gun pit accommodated a 3.7in heavy artillery gun. To the north of the site was hutting for the accommodation of the battery personnel. When the gun battery went into disuse the hutting was used for a prisoner of war camp. The hutting has since been demolished.

The four gun pits and command building are in good condition, and the site is an excellent example of a Second World War heavy anti-aircraft battery.

AA07 Bannerhill HAA battery near Kenilworth, showing HAA gun pit 1 (September 2004).

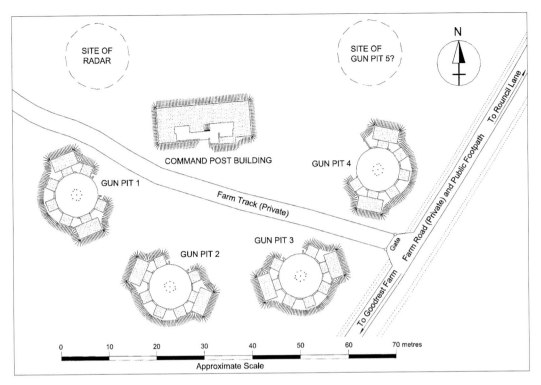

AA07 Bannerhill HAA battery near Kenilworth: site layout plan.

AA07 Bannerhill HAA battery near Kenilworth, showing the command post building (September 2004).

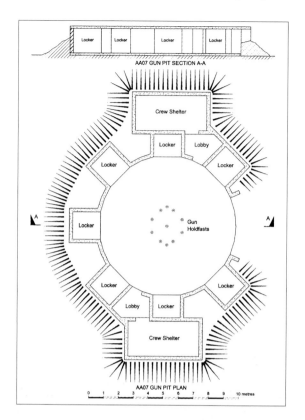

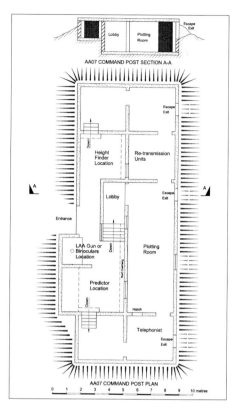

AA08 Light anti-aircraft battery sites at Leamington Spa

Light anti-aircraft gun batteries protected the railways and factories at Leamington Spa. The Lockheed factory on the south side of Leamington Spa was protected by LAA guns located on the office and factory roofs.

The anti-aircraft defences for Leamington Spa were coordinated from a headquarters located in a former house, The Gables, near the Kenilworth Road, north of Leamington Spa. The house is currently (as of 2004) private office accommodation.

There are no known visible remains of LAA batteries in Leamington Spa.

AA09 Stoneleigh HAA battery near Stoneleigh (NGR: SP329736)

This heavy anti-aircraft battery was located 500m south-east of Finham Bridge, near Stoneleigh. The site code H28 put it within the Coventry GDA. An aerial photograph from 1946 identified four gun pits and a command post building.

AA10 Searchlight battery near Long Itchington (NGR: 398645)

This searchlight battery, identified as three crop marks on aerial photographs, was located near Snowford Hill Farm, 0.75 miles south-east of Long Itchington. Excavations carried out in 1970 revealed sandbags.

Within 200m of the searchlight battery location, within a hedge (NGR: SP 397644), are the remains of what is locally reputed to be a carriage for a searchlight. Further investigation is required to verify whether it really is a searchlight carriage.

Opposite left: AA07 Bannerhill HAA battery near Kenilworth: gun pit 2 plan and section.

Opposite right: AA07 Bannerhill HAA battery near Kenilworth: command post building plan and section.

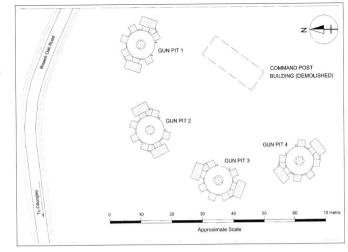

Right: AA14 Fillongley HAA battery: site layout plan.

AA14 Fillongley HAA battery: gun pits 1–4 (September 2004).

AA14 Fillongley HAA battery: gun pit 1 (September 2004).

AA11 Anti-aircraft battery near Lawford Heath (NGR: SP 45-72-)
Another light anti-aircraft battery was located on private farmland, 0.5 miles south of Lawford Heath, near the A45 trunk road. Three circular ring ditch crop marks were identified on aerial photographs.

AA12 Light anti-aircraft battery sites at Rugby
A defence ring of light anti-aircraft gun batteries protected the important railway junctions and factories at Rugby. Records indicate there were eight Bofors gun sites and eleven Lewis gun sites. Many of the sites are destroyed, but at several sites there are basic remains of concrete bases with holdfast fixings for Bofors guns.

Excellent information regarding the Rugby LAA battery sites is provided in the Warwickshire Sites and Monuments Record website, within the 'gun emplacements' search category: www.warwickshire.gov.uk/timetrail.

AA13 Anti-aircraft battery near Barnacle (NGR: SP 39-84-)
Site of a light anti-aircraft battery located on private farmland, this battery was situated 0.5 miles east of Barnacle, south of Bulkington. Four circular ring ditch crop marks were identified on aerial photographs.

AA14 'Fillongley' HAA battery near Fillongley (NGR: SP301871)
This was a four-gun heavy anti-aircraft battery located on private farmland near High House Farm, Breach Oak Lane, 1 mile east of Fillongley. The site code of H27 put it within the Coventry GDA.

The battery consisted of four gun pits. During the Second World War each gun pit accommodated a 3.7in heavy artillery gun. The command post building has been demolished. The site plan layout is very similar to AA07, minor differences being that at AA14 the earth banks to the gun pits have been removed and the crew shelter lobbies have reinforced concrete roofs.

The four gun pits are in good condition, but are being modified with blockwork additions for use as stables and housings for farm animals (September 2004).

AA15 Searchlight battery near Hurley (NGR: SP 24-95-)
Searchlight battery located on private farmland, 0.5 miles north-east of Foul End, south of Hurley and east of Kingsbury. There are no visible remains.

AA16 to AA30 Coventry heavy anti-aircraft batteries (NGR: Various)
By the end of the Second World War the Coventry Gun Defended Area (GDA) had approximately eighteen designated HAA battery sites. Previous references AA07, AA09 and AA14 describe three of these sites. Refer to Appendix 2, Warwickshire Anti-Aircraft Defences Gazetteer for the locations of HAA battery sites AA16 to AA30. No known visible remains exist at these locations.

6

Second World War Bombing Decoy Sites

Introduction

Bombing decoy sites were constructed to deceive and divert enemy bombers from attacking the intended targets. An Air Ministry department, directed by a Colonel Turner, generally undertook the design and construction of decoys. The department was initially based on the Strand in London, but, during 1940 they moved to Sound City at Shepperton. A Civil Defence Camouflage Establishment based at Leamington Spa also undertook experiments in decoy design, while aircraft based at RAF Baginton recorded photographs of the decoys. During 1940 the research undertaken by the Leamington Spa establishment was pooled with Colonel Turner's department and this department became responsible for the overall design and coordination of decoys nationally.

The following are the main types of bombing decoy sites provided during the Second World War:

Type K site:	Daytime bombing decoy to simulate an airfield
Type Q site:	Night-time bombing decoy for an airfield
Type QF site:	Night-time bombing decoy using mock fires
Type QL site:	Night-time bombing decoy to simulate permitted lighting
Type SF site:	Night-time bombing decoy to simulate burning of an urban site (Also known as 'Special Fire' or 'Starfish')
Type M site:	Dummy buildings

The type Q night bombing decoy for airfields generally comprised a dummy runway with a system of ground lighting and/or fires. Several type Q sites were constructed in Warwickshire during the Second World War.

Following the devastating bombing of Coventry during November 1940, additional type SF, QF and QL bombing decoy sites were constructed for many major cities and towns. These sites were located in areas of large open land and generally there are few surviving remains. The only substantial structure was the combined control shelter and generator building. This building was normally located some distance from the decoy (365m or 400 yards) and usually had brickwork walls, concrete roof and earthen banks. The control shelter typically had cable ducting, small observation ports and a roof observation/emergency escape hatch.

Warwickshire Bombing Decoy Sites

The following are examples of Warwickshire bombing decoy sites:

BD01 Pillerton Priors type Q site (NGR: SP 309480)

The RAF operated a type Q bombing decoy site 1 mile north-east of Pillerton Priors. The site comprised a dummy runway with ground landing lights and was used as a decoy for bombers seeking RAF Wellesbourne Mountford, 5.5 miles further to the north-east. To the south-east of Pillerton Hersey (NGR: SP 309476) is a small building which looks to have been constructed around the time of the Second World War. It may have housed generators for the dummy ground landing lights but is now disused. In more recent years the building was used as a diesel pump-house for water supply. Further research is required to verify that the building was used to house a generator for the decoy site. The building's internal dimensions are 2200mm x 1400mm x 2050mm high, with 225mm-thick brick walls and a concrete roof with a 600mm x 400mm roof hatch.

BD02 Wolverton type Q site (NGR: SP 218616)

This type Q bombing decoy site was located 900m south-east of Wolverton. The site was used as a decoy for bombers seeking RAF Honiley, 7 miles north and/or RAF Snitterfield, 1.5 miles south-west. There are no known surviving remains of this installation.

BD03 Wootton Wawen type Q site (NGR: SP 129611)

Site of a type Q bombing decoy site, located 2 miles south-west of Wootton Wawen, 1000m west of Little Alne. The site was used as a decoy for bombers seeking RAF Honiley, which lay 9.5 miles north-east and/or RAF Snitterfield, 4.5 miles east. There are no known surviving remains.

BD04 Hunningham type SF, QF and QL site (NGR: SP 364676)

This decoy site was located 1 mile south-west of Hunningham. The site had facilities for an extended grid of ground lights and fires acting as a decoy for bombers seeking Coventry, located 10 miles north. The combined control shelter and generator building is located adjacent to a bridleway, WNW of Fields Farm, Hunningham (NGR: SP 364672). The building housed generators and control equipment for the extended grid of ground lights and fires. Two concrete bases for generators exist within the building (as of 2004).

BD05 Eathorpe type QL site (NGR: SP 395680)

Another decoy site, this time located 0.75 miles south of Eathorpe. The site was used as a decoy for Coventry 8 miles NNW. There are no known visible remains.

BD06 Leamington Hastings type SF, QL and M site (NGR: SP 450680)

This decoy site was located 0.5 miles north-east of Leamington Hastings. The site was a decoy for Coventry, 10 miles to the north-west, and also for the Armstrong-Whitworth (AW) aircraft factory at Baginton, sited 7 miles north-west of its decoy. The type M was a daytime decoy comprising a dummy factory designed and constructed to replicate the AW aircraft factory buildings. The M decoy was constructed in the summer of 1940 and eventually closed during June 1942 when the decision was taken that daytime decoys were uneconomic and that henceforth decoys were to be operated almost exclusively during the night.

BD04 Control and generator building near Hunningham (September 2003).

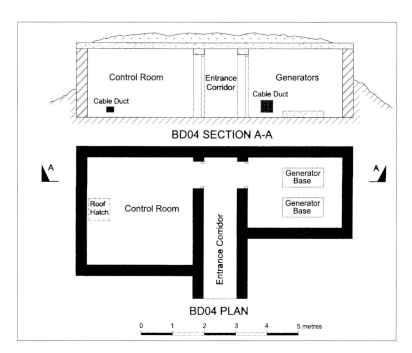

BD04 Control and generator building near Hunningham: plan and section.

The combined control shelter and generator building is located on strictly private farmland between the villages of Hill and Kites Hardwick (NGR: SP 463674). During the year 2000 the building was recorded to be in poor condition and the roof had been demolished.

BD07 Bubbenhall type QF and QL site (NGR: SP 358706)

This decoy site was located 1 mile south of Bubbenhall. It acted as one of Coventry's many decoys. There are no known visible remains.

BD08 Control and generator
building near Brandon
(September 2003).

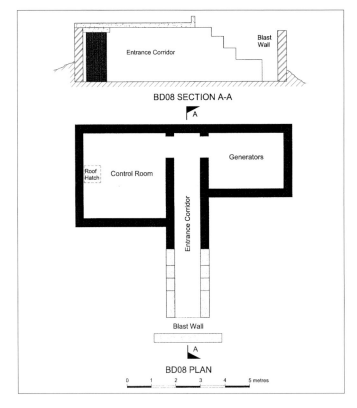

BD08 Control and generator
building near Brandon: plan
and section.

BD08 Bretford type SF site (NGR: SP 418777)

Decoy site located 0.75 miles to the west of Bretford. The site had facilities for fires which acted as a decoy, again for bombers seeking Coventry, 4 miles to the west. The combined control shelter and generator building is located adjacent to a public footpath, 0.5 miles north-east of Brandon (NGR: SP 414769). The building housed generators and control equipment for the decoy fires.

BD09 Control and generator building near Meriden (June 2004).

BD09 Meriden type QF and QL site (NGR: SP 272829)

This decoy site was located 1.5 miles north-east of Meriden, near Couchman's Farm. It is within the metropolitan county of West Midlands, although prior to the reorganisation of local government in 1974, BD09 was within the Warwickshire boundary. The site had facilities for an extended grid of ground lights and fires acting as a decoy for bombers seeking Coventry, 4 miles to the south-east.

The combined control shelter and generator building for the decoy site is located adjacent to a public footpath, 2 miles north-east of Meriden (NGR: SP 275833). The building housed generators and control equipment for the extended grid of ground lights and fires. The basic room layout of the building is the same as BD04 and BD08 with the main difference being the entrance blast walls, which are made of triangular-shaped reinforced concrete.

The emergency escape hatch steel cat ladder and hatch brick upstand on the roof exist (2004).

BD10 Astley type QL site (Not traced)

Another decoy site for Coventry located to the north of the city. Its precise location has not been traced.

BD11 Wibtoft type Q site (NGR: SP 468864)

This was another decoy site located 1 mile to the south of Wibtoft. The site had facilities for an extended grid of simulated airfield ground lights as a decoy for bombers seeking RAF Bramcote, which lay 4 miles to the west.

The combined control shelter and generator building for the decoy site is located in a field adjacent to a minor road between Cloudesley Bush and Wibtoft (NGR: SP 468864). The building housed generators and control equipment for the extended grid of simulated airfield ground lights. The decoy may have been simulating a system of airfield lighting known as Drem Lighting. This system comprised runway lighting, a flare path, angle of approach lighting, circuit lighting and perimeter track taxiing lighting.

One end wall and the internal walls have been demolished to convert the building into a shelter for farm animals.

BD12 to BD14 Decoy sites for Rugby and Nuneaton (NGR: Various)

The two type SF and QL decoy sites for Rugby were named Barby and Clay Coton and a type QL decoy site for Nuneaton was named Shenton. Refer to Appendix 2, Warwickshire Defences

BD11 Control and generator
building near Wibtoft (June 2006).

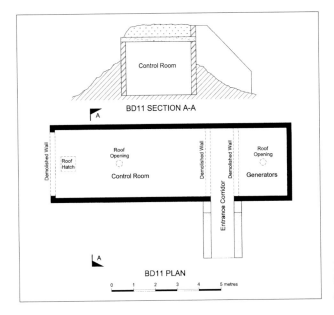

BD11 Control and generator
building near Wibtoft: plan and
section.

Gazetteer for national grid references and locations. There are no known visible remains at any
of these three decoy sites.

BD15 to BD22 Decoy sites for Birmingham (NGR: Various)

The type SF, Q, QF and QL decoy sites for Birmingham, named Halford, Moreton Bagot,
Mappleborough, Maxstoke and Kingsbury respectively, were located within Warwickshire while
Balsall, Bickenhill and Overgreen were within the West Midlands' county boundary.

Refer to Appendix 2, Warwickshire Defences Gazetteer for national grid references and
locations. There are no known visible remains at any of these eight decoy sites.

In addition to the above, there were also fourteen decoy sites for Birmingham located in
Worcestershire, Shropshire and Staffordshire. The names of the SF sites were Holt End, Fairfield,
Peopleton and Silvington. The QF and QL sites were Newton, Little Aston, Great Barr,
Alvechurch, Illey, Stourbridge, Uphampton, Shrawley, Ribbesford and Tile Cross.

7

Second World War
Air-Raid Shelters

Introduction

During the Second World War, Coventry and Birmingham were vital industrial centres for the production of military aircraft, vehicles and military components. Both cities were prime targets for German bombing attacks. The 1937 Air Raid Precautions Act resulted in a statutory requirement for local governments to provide protection for the civilian population.

Further to the legislation cited above, the following types of air-raid shelters were provided in Warwickshire during the Second World War:

> Military personnel shelters at RAF airfields
> Communal shelters at towns, factories, offices, schools and hospitals
> Domestic shelters for civilians

Military Personnel Shelters at RAF Airfields

A common type was the Stanton air-raid shelter, constructed of modular pre-cast concrete panels with a cross-sectional parabolic shape. The shelters were generally partially underground with an earth mound covering. The plan shape was rectangular and had an entrance with steps at one end and an emergency exit at the other. The emergency exit consisted of a concrete or brickwork vertical shaft fitted with a cat ladder.

Other examples of shelter types at RAF airfields were open trench shelters, covered trench shelters and blast shelters. Blast type shelters consisted of open enclosures (no roofs) with brickwork retaining walls surrounded with earth embankments. Normally there would have been two entrances.

Communal Shelters

Communal shelters were built for towns, factories, offices, schools and hospitals. The most common types were surface-built single storey shelters constructed with brick walls and reinforced concrete roofs. Within the Coventry boundary there were approximately eighty communal shelters capable of providing shelter for nearly 30,000 people. The majority of these shelters have since been demolished.

Domestic Shelters for Civilians

Communal shelters were not very popular, and so the Government offered domestic shelters to individual households. The standard external type was the Anderson shelter, which was offered at a cost of £7, or free to households with an income of less than £250 per annum. Anderson shelters were surface mounted or partially underground. The construction was of curved corrugated sheeting covered over with soil or sandbags to provide bomb blast protection. The majority of Warwickshire Anderson shelters have been destroyed, but some still exist in the back gardens of Coventry and Birmingham.

During late 1941 the Morrison shelter was produced, this model was designed for indoor use and was favoured by many families who preferred to shelter within their homes. Other proprietary designs were steel Consol shelters and pre-cast concrete Raidsafe shelters.

Warwickshire Air-Raid Shelters

The following are examples of Warwickshire air-raid shelter sites:

AR01 Stanton air-raid shelter at Southam (NGR: SP 425613)
This partially underground Stanton AR shelter is located 0.75 miles south-east of Southam, in private allotments adjacent to the Welsh Road to Priors Marston. RAF personnel at the former RAF Southam Airfield would have originally used the shelter. The shelter is currently utilised as storage space for the allotment users.

AR02 Domestic air-raid shelter at Clifton upon Dunsmore (NGR: SP 531764)
This rectangular surface air-raid shelter was built on the west side of Church Street, Clifton upon Dunsmore. Construction is solid brickwork walls and reinforced concrete roof. There is one entrance door and a single airbrick in each end wall.

AR03 Domestic air-raid shelter at Clifton upon Dunsmore (NGR: SP 528762)
Square surface air-raid shelter located in a private garden, adjacent to a row of terraced houses, opposite the village school on South Road, Clifton upon Dunsmore. The construction is of solid brickwork walls with a reinforced concrete roof. There is one entrance door and a single airbrick in one wall and the shelter is well concealed by ivy.

AR04 Kenilworth air-raid shelters (NGR: Various)
Communal air-raid shelters for civilians were located at various locations in Kenilworth.
The following are examples of Kenilworth underground communal air-raid shelters. At each location the earth mound is visible (as of 2004), and at the first four locations the entrance is visible but remains closed with post-1945 brickwork.
AR04a: Abbey Fields adjacent to Forrest Road (NGR: SP 284720)
Mound and entrance with exposed concrete roof to the entrance which is located near the junction with Borrowell Lane.

AR01 Stanton shelter at Southam (July 2004).

AR02 Domestic air-raid shelter at Clifton upon Dunsmore (September 2004).

AR04b: Abbey Fields adjacent to Rosemary Hill (NGR: SP 288722)

The mound and entrance are diagonally opposite the Priory Theatre. There is an exposed, angled concrete roof to the entrance.

AR04c: Abbey Fields adjacent to Bridge Street AR (NGR: SP 286725)

The mound and entrance are visible opposite the Abbotsford School and they are located in the corner of the Abbey Fields car park. Part of the roof escape hatch's concrete surrounds are also visible.

AR04d: New Street (NGR: SP 288727)

The mound and entrance are to be found diagonally opposite the Royal Oak public house.

AR04e: Castle Road (NGR: SP 279724)

This shelter was located within the mound outside Kenilworth Castle, on the opposite side of the road to Castle Green. The shelter entrance was condemned as unsightly and so demolished during March 1974.

Further recorded locations of air-raid shelters in Kenilworth include Saint Augustine's School in Beehive Lane, the green in Hyde Road, junction of Arthur Street and Spring Lane, by Saint John's church hall, Saint Nicholas' School grounds, by the former cinema in Station Road, and an ARP headquarters under Park Hill Bridge.

AR05 Stanton air-raid shelter at former RAF Wellesbourne Mountford (NGR: SP 55-26)

Site of Stanton air-raid shelter near the north-east boundary of former RAF Wellesbourne Mountford Airfield. The shelter was destroyed during recent building redevelopment works.

AR06 Stanton air-raid shelter at former RAF Stratford (NGR: SP 211512)

Partially underground Stanton air-raid shelter located in a wood, adjacent to a public footpath, near the A3400 road by the western perimeter of former RAF Stratford.

AR07 Blast air-raid shelter at former RAF Stratford (NGR: SP 218515)

Blast air-raid shelter located on private farmland to the east of Ailstone Farm, within former RAF Stratford. There are two entrances to the shelter brickwork wall enclosures, and the overall enclosure is surrounded by earth embankments. After the end of the war the internal enclosures were infilled with soil.

AR08 Stanton air-raid shelter, at former RAF Stratford (NGR: SP 218522)

Located partially underground, this Stanton air-raid shelter is in the middle of private farmland, adjacent to a public footpath, near the northern perimeter of former RAF Stratford.

AR08 Stanton air-raid shelter at former RAF Stratford (December 2003).

AR09 Stanton air-raid shelter at former RAF Long Marston (NGR: SP 176492)
Surface Stanton air-raid shelter located on private farmland near the north-eastern perimeter of former RAF Long Marston.

AR10 Stanton air-raid Shelter, Long Marston Airfield (NGR: SP 180492)
Surface Stanton air-raid shelter located on private farmland in a dispersed site on the opposite side of the B4632 road to the airfield.

AR10 Stanton air-raid shelter at former RAF Long Marston. External view with mound removed (August 2006).

AR10 Stanton air-raid shelter at former RAF Long Marston. Interior showing ribbed concrete panels (August 2006).

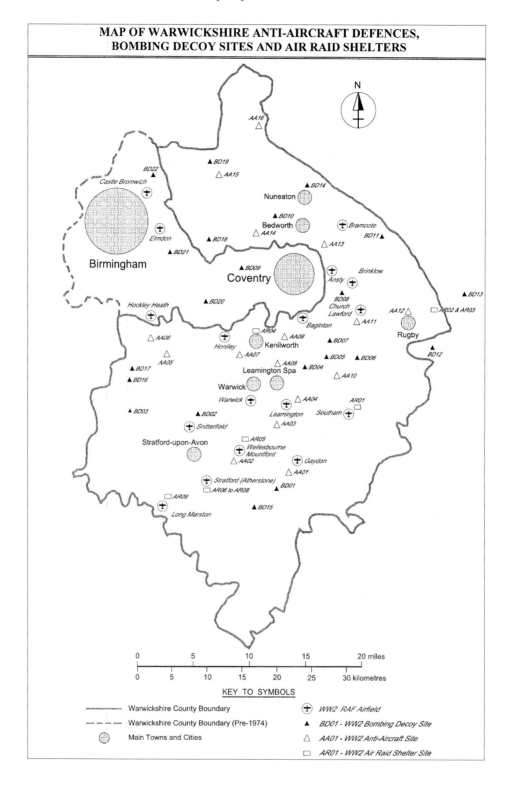

MAP OF WARWICKSHIRE ANTI-AIRCRAFT DEFENCES, BOMBING DECOY SITES AND AIR RAID SHELTERS

N

AA16

BD19
AA15

BD22
Castle Bromwich

BD14

Nuneaton

BD10
Bedworth
AA14

Bramcote
BD11

Elmdon

BD18

AA13

BD21

Birmingham

BD09

Coventry

Brinklow

Ansty

BD13

Hockley Heath

BD20

BD08
Church
Lawford

AA12

AR02 & AR03

Baginton

AA11

AR04

Rugby

AA06

AA09

Honiley

Kenilworth

BD07

BD12

AA07

AA05

AA08

BD05

BD06

BD17

Leamington Spa

AA10

BD16

BD04

Warwick

Warwick

AA04

AR01

BD03

BD02

Leamington

Southam

Snitterfield

AA03

AR05

Stratford-upon-Avon

Wellesbourne
Mountford

AA02

Gaydon

AA01

Stratford (Atherstone)

BD01

AR06 to AR08

AR09

BD15

Long Marston

0   5   10   15   20 miles

0 5 10 15 20 25 30 kilometres

KEY TO SYMBOLS

‒‒‒‒‒‒	Warwickshire County Boundary
‒ ‒ ‒	Warwickshire County Boundary (Pre-1974)
⊕	Main Towns and Cities
⊕	WW2 RAF Airfield
▲	BD01 - WW2 Bombing Decoy Site
△	AA01 - WW2 Anti-Aircraft Site
☐	AR01 - WW2 Air Raid Shelter Site

8

Army Buildings and Structures

Introduction

Whilst this section concentrates mainly on army buildings and structures it is important to briefly describe some of the army regiments associated with Warwickshire:

The Royal Warwickshire Regiment
The Warwickshire Regiment was awarded the title 'Royal' in 1832 and has served the nation in conflicts across the globe. In 1963 the regiment was renamed the Royal Warwickshire Fusiliers and in 1968 it merged with three other fusilier regiments to form the Royal Regiment of Fusiliers. The Royal Regiment of Fusiliers Museum (Royal Warwickshire) is located in St John's House, Warwick.

The Warwickshire Yeomanry
Formed in 1794 during the Napoleonic Wars. In 1958 it merged with the Queen's Own Worcestershire Hussars to form the Queen's Own Warwickshire and Worcestershire Yeomanry before being reduced to two squadrons in 1969. The Warwickshire Yeomanry Museum is located in the basement of the Court House, Jury Street, Warwick.

The Queen's Own Hussars
West Midlands' cavalry regiment was originally formed in 1685. The successor to the Queen's Own Hussars is the Queen's Royal Hussars. The Queen's Own Hussars Museum is located on the first floor of the Medieval Guildhall of the Lord Leycester Hospital, High Street, Warwick.

Army Barracks and Depots

Summary of the active and closed Warwickshire principal army barracks and army depots and their current status (as of 2006):

> Budbrooke Barracks, Warwick (demolished 1960)
> Gamecock Barracks, Bramcote (active MoD army barracks)
> Kineton Depot (active MoD depot)

Long Marston Depot (MoD depot closed and now used for private sector storage)
The Czechoslovak Brigade Billets (headquarters demolished)

The following is a brief history of each of the above sites and examples of the buildings and structures that were located there:

Budbrooke Barracks, Warwick
Budbrooke Barracks was located 2 miles west of Warwick. The barracks were constructed *c.*1876 and during the early twentieth century additional buildings were constructed. The principal buildings were accommodation blocks, married soldiers' quarters, a hospital, stores and administration buildings.

During the First World War the barracks' main role was army recruitment and despatching men to various battalions in the British Isles for training. At this time the training of soldiers was not undertaken at the barracks.

During the Second World War infantry recruitment and training took place at the barracks. After hostilities had ceased the barracks were a depot for the Royal Warwickshire Regiment while also handling National Service recruits. In March 1948 the name changed to the Midland Brigade Training Centre, although from 1950 onwards the site was slowly run down, during and 1960 the last remaining army units were moved to Glen Parva, Leicestershire. The barracks officially closed on 10 August 1960. The majority of buildings were demolished and Hampton Magna village now occupies the site.

One remnant of the Budbrooke Barracks is the remains of the shooting range wall (NGR: SP254648).

ABD01 Shooting range wall at site of former Budbrooke Barracks (March 2006).

ABD02 Modern barracks at Gamecock Army Barracks (September 2006).

Gamecock Barracks, Bramcote

Gamecock Barracks, 3 miles south-east of Nuneaton, was originally the site of the RAF Bramcote base that was constructed 1939/40. In late 1946 RAF Bramcote was taken over by the Royal Navy and became known as Royal Navy Air Station HMS *Gamecock*. The main function of HMS *Gamecock* was technical training for naval airmen and aircraft mechanics as well as providing a centre for the Royal Naval Voluntary Reserve (RNVR Air branch), 1833 Squadron. The principal aircraft flown were Seafires, Fireflies and Sea Furies. During October 1955, 1833 Squadron was moved to RAF Honiley to be equipped with jet aircraft.

During 1959 the barracks were taken over by the Junior Leaders Regimental Royal Artillery. The barracks became the home of the 30th Signal Regiment in September 1993.

The principal buildings at Gamecock Barracks are barracks accommodation, married quarters, stores, workshops and training facilities. The original buildings at Bramcote were built to a higher specification than wartime buildings because RAF Bramcote was one of the last Expansion Period stations approved prior to 1939. Refer to the RAF Airfields and Buildings section for descriptions of buildings surviving from the RAF Bramcote era.

Kineton Depot

The Kineton Depot, 2 miles east of Kineton, was originally planned in 1941 to hold 100000 tons of ammunition. By the end of the war the depot was holding 137000 tons in 252 explosives store houses. Within the depot was an extensive railway network with a branch line connection to the London to Birmingham line at Fenny Compton.

In the post-war years the depot was extensively altered, and a site visit report undertaken in 1999 indicated that only six out of the original 252 explosive houses remained. The original buildings were replaced with new buildings and facilities.

The name of the depot has been altered on a number of occasions and sample names are as follows:

CAD Kineton (Central Ammunition Depot)
BAD Kineton (Base Ammunition Depot)
DMC Kineton (Defence Munitions Centre, current name)

The current depot has extensive facilities on both sides of the B4086 Kineton to Warmington Road, with Edgehill sub-depot south of the B4086 and the Marlborough sub-depot to the north. Examples of the depot facilities include ammunition storage buildings, ammunition process buildings, barracks, married quarters, teaching blocks, maintenance buildings, motor transport buildings and mess facilities. The original railway network has been reduced in size but still serves the majority of the depot, while various railway stations remain in existence.

The majority of buildings at Kineton Depot are storage buildings for ammunition and explosives. Explosives storage buildings are designed and constructed specifically to limit the possibility of an accidental explosion, limit the spread of an explosion, limit injury to personnel and limit damage to adjacent facilities. Protection is generally achieved by rigorous standards of construction and by spacing the buildings at sufficient distances to limit explosion effects. The two principal types of explosives storage buildings at Kineton are Standard Explosives Store House (SESH) and Igloo buildings.

SESH buildings are located above ground and the construction is of brick and reinforced concrete walls with reinforced concrete roofs and heavy steel doors. The construction is intended to provide sufficient protection from the effects of an external explosion while the separation distances between buildings achieve additional protection.

Igloo buildings are located above ground and the construction is of reinforced concrete with a curved roof and earth cover. Entrance doors are heavy steel in their construction. The structure is designed to resist blast effects without collapse.

Another building type is the Ammunition Process Building (APB) in which ammunition and explosives are serviced. Construction is of brick and reinforced concrete. Earth embankments to minimise blast effects are used to surround APB buildings.

Long Marston Depot

The Long Marston depot was originally constructed as an army camp during 1940/1941 at the same time as the construction of RAF Long Marston. Many of the buildings were temporary and were replaced in the immediate post-war years with various brick buildings and large storage shed facilities for use by the Royal Engineers. The depot was known for many years as the Royal Engineers Central Engineering Park (CEP).

The Royal Engineers vacated the depot on 1 April 1999 and the site storage facilities are now leased to private companies. The majority of the MoD buildings are retained and are in good condition.

Drill Halls and Territorial Army Centres

Drill halls for the training of military personnel were located in the majority of Warwickshire towns. Yeomanry Hall was the original name of a number of the drill halls, named after the yeomanry volunteer cavalry force, which was originally formed in the eighteenth century for home defence. The Yeomanry merged with the Territorial Force in 1907 and is now known as the Territorial Army (TA).

Refer to Appendix 2 for examples and locations of Warwickshire drill halls and Territorial Army Centres.

The Home Guard

The Local Defence Volunteers (LDV) was officially created in May 1940 and renamed as the Home Guard in July 1940. During the war the Home Guard played an important role in supporting the Regular Army by carrying out observation duties, occupying defensive positions such as roadblocks, anti-tank islands, defended localities and providing defence against potential airborne landings. The Home Guard was also assigned agreed tasks to assist the Civil Defence Services before, during and after air raids. These tasks included dealing with incendiary bombs, rescue work, ambulance work, fire-watching, message duties, warden's duties, clearing blocked streets, evacuation of bombed areas and traffic control. ·

Home Guard battalions were set up and trained throughout Warwickshire. The boundaries between Home Guard sectors were the previously established boundaries of the Warwickshire County and City Constabulary divisions. Buildings primarily utilised by the Home Guard were village halls, police stations, drill halls, school halls, public houses and church towers for observation purposes.

The photograph below is a classic example of the early days of a LDV unit prior to the change in name to the Home Guard. The unit was Warwickshire No.4 Platoon within 'A' Sector (initially designated Rugby Division). Research indicates that the vicar pictured holding a First World War rifle was the Revd A. Wilbraham of Marton. The armoured vehicle was constructed on the chassis of a Morris commercial lorry converted at a factory in Warwick. The armoured body consisted of a 6mm welded steel plate fitted with embrasures for small arms fire. On the stand down of the Home Guard in November 1944 the armoured vehicle vanished.

The following table provides an example of the structure and roles of a Warwickshire Home Guard Battalion and is compiled from original Home Guard documents.

Warwickshire No.4 Platoon Local Defence Volunteers, *c*.1940. (Courtesy of the *Coventry Evening Telegraph*)

4th BATTALION WARWICK HOME GUARD		
Battalion Headquarters (Ordinary): Yeomanry Hall, Stratford		
Battalion Headquarters (Operational): 26 Bridge Street, Stratford		
Battalion Commander: Lt Col G.M. Bryant		
COMPANY OR PLATOON	HEADQUARTERS	MAIN ROLE
'A' Company	15 Henley Street, Alcester.	Hold Alcester as a defended locality with 9 Platoon (900 men).
'B' Company	Binton	Defend the Alcester Road and Evesham Road into Stratford (300 to 400 men).
'C' Company	Yeomanry Hall, Stratford	Defend Stratford, two zones north and south of the river Avon. Each zone under one officer. Roadblocks on all approach roads.
'D' Company		Operational role was counter attack and defence of Stratford.
Platoon D1	Parish Hall, Tiddington	
Platoon D2	Village Hall, Snitterfield	
Platoon D3	Institute Hall, Hampton Lucy	
Platoon D4	The School, Loxley	
'E' Company		
3 Platoon	Bridge Street, Kineton	Roadblock on the Banbury to Stratford Road near Sun Rising Hill.
4 Platoon	Warmington churchyard	Roadblock on the Banbury to Stratford Road near Warmington Hill.
'F' Company	Police Station, Shipston-on-Stour	Mobile.
1 Platoon		Defence of Oxford Road/ Fosse Way road junction near Tredington.

Note: Above information compiled from Home Guard documents dated 7 July 1943 and stored in the Warwickshire County Record Office.

The Czechoslovak Brigade Billets

Following the fall of France in 1940, Czechoslovak troops were evacuated from the south of France to England. The troops were initially based at a tented camp in Cheshire. In October 1940 the troops were moved to mid-Warwickshire, where they were based until relocation to Dorset in May 1942. The Czechoslovak Brigade headquarters were at Harrington House, Newbold Terrace, Leamington Spa. Harrington House was demolished in the 1960s and the Royal Spa Centre now occupies the site. The troops were billeted in Leamington Spa, Warwick and south Warwickshire villages including Barford, Wellesbourne, Moreton Morrell, Kineton and Butlers Marston. The large country houses of Walton Hall, Friz Hill House at Walton, Moreton Hall and Moreton Paddox, were also requisitioned and temporary hutted accommodation was erected in the grounds. Moreton Paddox was demolished after the end of the war.

The Czechoslovak memorial fountain in the Jephson Gardens, Leamington Spa, commemorates, in particular, the seven volunteers from the Free Czechoslovak forces stationed in Leamington Spa who parachuted into their homeland to assassinate the SS General Heydrich. The memorial represents a falling parachute and streams of water form the parachute strings.

Prisoner of War Camps

Prisoner of war camps were built throughout the British Isles during the Second World War to accommodate military prisoners captured by the Allies. Up until 1942 the number of prisoners captured by British forces was relatively small and consisted mainly of Luftwaffe aircrews and naval personnel. From 1942 onwards (following the North African campaign) the PoW numbers steadily increased. To cope with the PoW influx, contracts were placed with various major building contractors to construct camps to standard designs. A typical PoW camp would have consisted of a guards' complex and prisoners' compound. The guards' complex would have typically consisted of officers' and soldiers' accommodation, administration offices, storage buildings and an elevated water storage tank. The prisoners' compound typically consisted of accommodation huts, dining and recreation huts, workshops, ablution huts and camp reception station (CRS). The CRS consisted of sick bay rooms, medical officers' facilities, offices, stores, ablutions and a kitchen.

PoW camps were built rapidly and were intended only as temporary short life structures. Many of the buildings were prefabricated huts consisting of standard panels produced in factories.

Examples of prefabricated hut types provided at PoW camps were Nissen huts, timber huts, British Concrete Federation (BCF) huts, Orlit huts and Ministry of Works (MoW) standard huts. For descriptions of these hut types refer to the sub-section within RAF Airfields and Buildings.

The Appendix 2 Warwickshire Defences Gazetteer lists the names and site locations of former prisoner of war camps in Warwickshire. The list is not comprehensive. The majority of buildings have been demolished and the land returned to agricultural use. The PW11 Stoneleigh Camp was located adjacent to an emergency military hospital used during the conflict. Many of the brick buildings constructed during the war for the hospital accommodation survive and are now let for office and storage usage.

PW15 Ladbroke prisoner of war camp and refugee camp – PoW camp MoW standard concrete hut (June 2006).

PW15 Ladbroke prisoner of war and refugee camp. 16ft and 32ft Nissen huts (June 2006).

PW15 Ladbroke Prisoner of War and Refugee Camp (NGR: SP421586)

Ladbroke PoW camp accommodated German and Italian PoWs and was located in Radbourne Lane, Ladbroke, 2.5 miles south of Southam. The PoW camp was a working camp and a number of the prisoners worked at the local Southam cement works. Immediately after the end of the war the camp was expanded to accommodate refugees and later became known locally as the Polish Camp.

During 1984 the refugee camp was finally closed and the majority of buildings have since been demolished. However, one MoW standard concrete hut survives from the PoW camp and two Nissen huts from the refugee camp era survive adjacent to the concrete hut.

9

Cold War Defences

Introduction

The Cold War period is generally recorded as commencing in 1947 and ending at either the fall of the Berlin Wall on 11 November 1989 or the end of the Soviet Union on 25 December 1991. Fortunately, 'hot' hostilities did not occur between the two superpowers, the USA and Soviet Union, and so the Cold War took the form of an arms race to acquire conventional and nuclear weapons, conducted through espionage, propaganda, trade embargoes and military alliances. One of the main features of the nuclear arms race was Mutually Assured Destruction or MAD, whereby it was considered the East would not attack the West, or vice versa, because of the potency of weapons possessed by both sides. And in any case the target of any such attack would still have time to launch a response on the initial aggressor.

Great Britain was heavily involved in the Cold War, and defence installations were constructed throughout the country. The following details examples of defence installations associated with the Cold War in Warwickshire.

RAF Gaydon V-Bomber Base

RAF Gaydon opened in June 1942 as a base for night bomber training. The airfield was provided with three runways in the conventional 'A' pattern layout. Other main facilities included a perimeter track with aircraft hard standings, two hangars (Type B1 and T2), and standard Second World War bomber training base buildings. During August 1946 the base was placed under care and maintenance.

RAF Gaydon was selected to become a V-bomber base and was completely reconstructed between 1953 and 1954. Sections of the Second World War runways were broken up and used as hardcore for a new, single 2743m-long (3000-yard) runway with parallel taxiway, access tracks and aircraft hard standings. The majority of the Second World War buildings were replaced with new structures including hangars, a control tower, technical, instructional, domestic, communal buildings and a remote atomic bomb store.

RAF Gaydon: eight Valiant V-bombers of No.138 Squadron, *c*.1956. (Courtesy of the *Leamington Times*)

RAF Gaydon re-opened on 1 March 1954 and No.3 Group Bomber Command was immediately stationed at the base. On 1 January 1955 the Valiant V-bomber entered service at RAF Gaydon with No.138 Squadron. RAF Gaydon became a training station for V-bomber crews and was known as the 'birth place of the RAF V-bomber force'. During November 1957 the Victor V-bomber entered service at RAF Gaydon. The Victor was the third of the new V-bombers, following the Valiant and Vulcan to complete Britain's V-bomber types.

V-bomber bases were at risk of pre-emptive attacks, and from 1958 onwards dispersal airfields were developed. RAF Pershore, Worcestershire, and RAF Bruntingthorpe, Leicestershire, are examples of dispersal airfields where armed bombers were sent at times of high international tension. A late addition to RAF Gaydon was the construction of an operational readiness platform (ORP). The ORP consisted of four hard standings at the end of the runway to enable bombers to take off at short notice.

In June 1965 the training of V-bomber crews ceased at RAF Gaydon and Britain's V-bomber forces were gradually reduced following the transfer of the main nuclear deterrent to the Royal Navy.

During 1970 the base was placed under care and maintenance and on 31 October 1974 RAF Gaydon was closed. British Leyland bought the base in 1974 and reconstructed the site as a vehicle testing and development centre. The runway and trackways were modified for use as test tracks. Embankments were built at the perimeter boundary and trees planted to reduce the risk of industrial espionage. The site is currently used by Ford as a design and test centre for Land Rover and Jaguar and also as a production centre for Aston Martin cars. The Heritage Motor Centre is also located on the site.

Various buildings survive from the V-bomber station era, including two Gaydon hangars, control tower, technical buildings, gymnasium, housing and atomic bomb store.

CW01 RAF Gaydon – Gaydon type hangars and a squadron of Hunter jet fighters in the late 1950s. (Courtesy of the *Leamington Times*)

CW01 RAF Gaydon – Gaydon type hangars where Hunter jet fighters once stood, *c.*2000. (Courtesy of the *Leamington Times*)

CW01 RAF Gaydon – Gaydon type hangars (NGR: SP 352549)

Two new purpose built hangars for V-bombers were constructed between 1953 and 1954 and were known as Gaydon hangars. This design type was constructed at other V-bomber bases. The Gaydon hangars are currently used as test and workshop facilities.

CW02 RAF Gaydon control tower (NGR: SP 348543)

The RAF Gaydon control tower was a post-Second World War, three-storey design known as a split vertical control type. Control of local aircraft movements was from a fully-glazed upper storey observation room and control of approach aircraft was from the floor below. The observation room glazing was angled to reduce reflections. The control tower is currently used as an observation tower for the Land Rover test centre complex.

CW03 RAF Gaydon atomic bomb store (NGR: SP 319544)

The RAF Gaydon atomic bomb store was built approximately 1 mile west of the airfield, at Lighthorne Rough. When it was constructed in the 1950s the main features of the facility were a compound with high security fencing, a guardroom, an assembly building, bomb storerooms and an external ancillary building. Partly assembled atomic bombs were delivered to the site and assembled in a Type D1 assembly building. The assembled bombs were then stored in Type D2 storerooms that were covered by earthwork banking. After the closure of RAF Gaydon the facility was used to store National Film Archives. New supplementary store buildings were constructed within the compound for the storage of films. The compound and the majority of the facility buildings survive, minus the atomic bombs!

CW02 RAF Gaydon control tower in the early 1970s. (Courtesy of Land Rover, Gaydon)

CW03 RAF Gaydon atomic bomb store. Entrance to compound and guardroom (August 2006).

CW03 RAF Gaydon atomic bomb store. External ancillary building (August 2006).

RAF Gaydon, an aerial view from south in the early 1970s. (Courtesy of Land Rover, Gaydon)

Key:

A	Main single runway
B	Taxiway
C	Dispersal platforms
D	Control tower
E	Compass platform
F	Gaydon hangars
G	Technical site
H	Domestic accommodation
I	Hangar
J	Operational readiness platform
K	Chadshunt village
L	Lighthorne village

Nuclear Attack Observation and Monitoring

The ROC and UKWMO Organisations

The Observer Corps was officially created in 1925 and in April 1941 it was retitled the Royal Observer Corps (ROC). The main role of the ROC was the identification and tracking of hostile aircraft from a network of observer posts located throughout Britain. Immediately after the end of the war the ROC was stood down, but it reformed in 1947 to continue in the role of tracking aircraft. In 1951 Orlit Ltd produced designs for two types of prefabricated concrete observation posts. The Orlit Type A was a ground level structure and the Orlit Type B was elevated on 1.83m (6ft) concrete posts with access via a ladder. Between 1952 and 1955 over 400 Orlit Posts were erected in Britain. Within Warwickshire no Orlit Posts survive.

With the increase in the speed of jet aircraft, the role of the ROC to effectively track aircraft began to diminish. During the 1950s the threat of nuclear attack increased and in 1955 the United Kingdom Warning and Monitoring Organisation (UKWMO) was formed and the ROC was given the added role of reporting nuclear bursts and monitoring radioactive fallout.

UMP10 Wolston nuclear attack ROC underground monitoring post (March 2006).

UMP12 Meriden nuclear attack ROC underground monitoring post (May 2006).

The five main functions of the UKWMO were:

1. Warning the public of any air attack
2. Confirming nuclear strikes
3. Warning the public of the approach of radioactive fallout
4. Providing the civilian and military authorities with details of nuclear bursts
5. Providing a post-attack meteorological service

In order to monitor and report nuclear attacks a national network of ROC underground monitoring posts and ROC group headquarters bunkers were constructed from 1957 onwards.

ROC Underground Monitoring Posts

The prototype underground monitoring post (UMP) was constructed in 1956 at Farnham, Surrey, and after incorporating minor modifications it became the standard construction design for the national network of over 1,500 underground monitoring posts. The UMPs were generally constructed at the existing site locations of the above ground ROC observer posts. The standard design UMP basically consisted of a buried reinforced concrete chamber

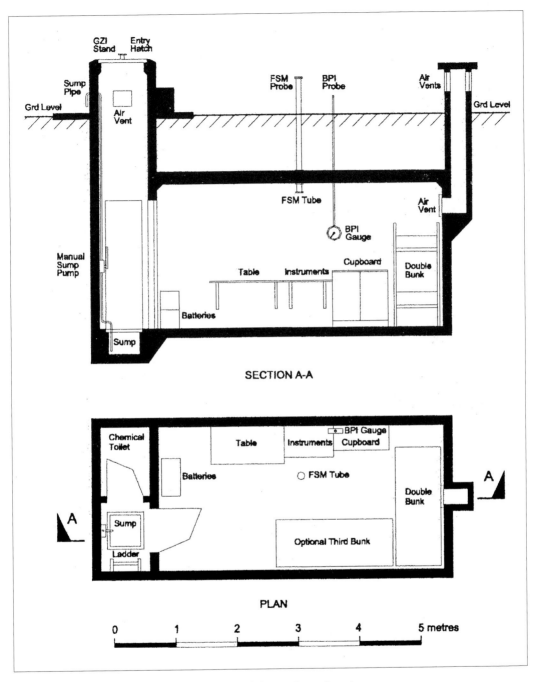

ROC underground monitoring post: standard design plan and section.

(approximate internal dimensions 5.6m x 2.3m x 2.3m) with a 4.5m-deep access shaft, monitoring room and storeroom with a chemical toilet.

Underground monitoring posts were equipped with the following principal monitoring instruments:

1. **Bomb Power Indicator (BPI)** – Measured the peak pressure of the blast wave and basically consisted of an above ground steel baffle plate linked via a steel pipe to a pressure indicator dial in the monitoring room.
2. **Ground Zero Indicator (GZI)** – Recorded the bearing and elevation of the fireball explosion and basically consisted of an above ground cylindrical pinhole camera unit with four chambers fitted with light sensitive paper. The unit was normally mounted on a pedestal by the entrance shaft and one member of the ROC team was designated to emerge from the UMP to retrieve the papers after an explosion!
3. **Fixed Survey Meter (FSM)** – Measured radiation levels and basically consisted of an above ground probe unit connected via a co-axial cable to a meter in the monitoring room.

Designated posts were also equipped with instruments to measure atmospheric pressure and temperature to enable meteorological reports to be produced.

Three ROC members staffed underground monitoring posts, while communication between posts and the group headquarters was conducted via telephone landlines. The posts were grouped in geographical clusters of three or four posts to enable the precise location of the detonation to be calculated by triangulation of monitoring data. In each cluster one post was designated master post and so was fitted with a VHF radio set. Master posts can be identified by the inclusion of a pneumatic aerial unit fitted to the side of the external air ventilator shaft.

Within Warwickshire, seventeen underground monitoring posts were constructed between 1959 and 1965. Five of these posts were decommissioned in 1968 and the remaining posts were operational until 1991 when the ROC was stood down. For a list of the names and locations of the Warwickshire ROC underground monitoring posts, refer to Appendix 2. Substantial remains survive at five of the UMP locations.

ROC Group Headquarters

Thirty-one ROC Group Headquarters were located nationally to control and collect data from the underground monitoring posts. Thirteen of the headquarters were new build surface buildings, twelve were new build semi-sunken buildings and six were located in existing ROC buildings. Five of the Group Headquarters were also designated Sector Headquarters. The headquarters were protected against nuclear blasts and designed to be self-sufficient for up to thirty days. They were provided with standby generators, air conditioning, emergency water supply, sleeping accommodation, food stores and catering facilities. One ROC Group Headquarters was located in Warwickshire at Lawford Heath.

CW04 Lawford Heath ROC Group Headquarters (NGR: SP 457736)

During the 1980s Warwickshire was part of the Midland Sector with the ROC Sector Headquarters located at Lincoln. The ROC Group Headquarters was designated Group No.8 Coventry and located at Lawford Heath, near Rugby. The building was a standard semi-sunken design consisting of a three level blockhouse surrounded by an earth mound. The exposed upper parts of the building were originally painted white to reflect the heat from nuclear flashes, but were later painted green in an effort to be less conspicuous.

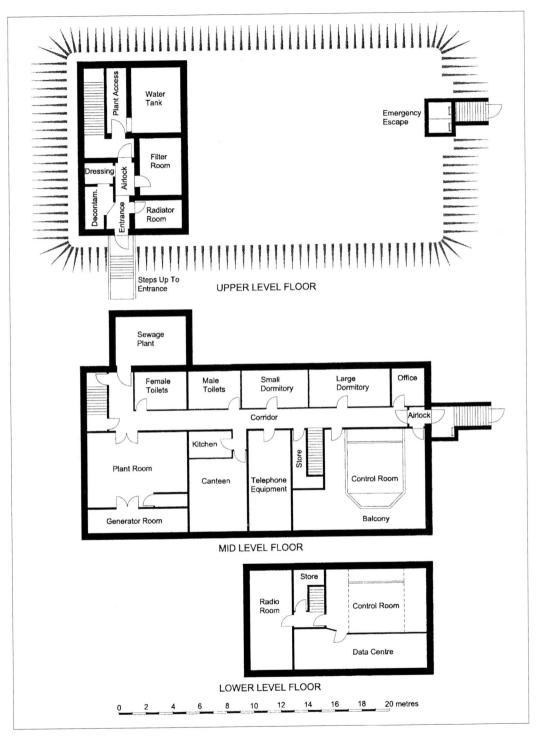

CW04 ROC Group Headquarters at Lawford Heath, Rugby. (Plans based on a drawing issued with the March 1994 sale auction documents.)

Lawford Heath ROC Group Headquarters was operational from 1963 to 1991. For a short period the site became Regional Government Headquarters No.9.2 and was considered as a replacement for the Regional Government Headquarters at Drakelow, Worcestershire. With the end of the Cold War the Home Office closed the site. The former headquarters were sold by auction in March 1994 and then resold to Satellite Media Services in 1997. The building was completely refurbished by Satellite Media Services and satellite communication dishes were erected adjacent to the original bunker. Currently the buildings are unoccupied and the future of the site is unknown.

Emergency Government Bunkers

Summary of the main categories and construction periods of Cold War government bunkers:

1. **Regional War Rooms (RWR) (1953 to 1956)** – Twelve Regional War Room bunkers were constructed nationwide to accommodate Regional Commissioners and support staff to organise civil defence and govern the region if central government was incapacitated. Warwickshire was within Region 9 of the Midlands with the RWR at Shirley, Birmingham.
2. **Regional Seats of Government (RSG) (mid-1950s to early 1960s)** – With the development of the hydrogen bomb Government policy was reviewed and regional seats of Government (RSG) planned. The headquarters bunker for each RSG was intended to provide accommodation for over 300 personnel and be sustainable for several months. Warwickshire was within Region 9 Midlands with the RSG facility located at Drakelow, near Kidderminster, in the Second World War underground aircraft engine factory.
3. **Sub Regional Headquarters (SRHQ) (1960s to 1966)** – SRHQs were planned to provide a close link to the local authorities and civil defence. Within Region 9 Midlands, one SRHQ bunker was constructed at Swynnerton, Staffordshire.
4. **Sub-Regional Controls (S-RC) (1966 to 1970s)** – This was a rationalisation of the SRGs and SRHQs following a Home Office directive in 1966. The majority of existing SRG and SRHQ bunkers were refurbished and adapted for use as S-RC bunkers.
5. **Regional Government Headquarters (RGHQ) (1980s)** – The Home Defence Review of 1980 recommended updated bunkers known as RGHQs. The Region 9 Midlands bunkers at Drakelow and Swynnerton were refurbished and Swynnerton took the lead role. In 1991 it was planned to close Drakelow and move the RGHQ to Lawford Heath, Warwickshire. With the end of the Cold War this move did not happen.
6. **County and Local Authority bunkers (1947 to 1991)** – The Home Office required local authorities to maintain protected emergency centres. The centres were generally in the basements of county halls. Home Office guidelines in the early 1970s required county councils to have two protected control centres consisting of one main centre known as the County Main and one remote standby bunker. The Warwickshire County Main bunker was at Wylde Green, near Sutton Coldfield, a facility originally used as anti-aircraft operations rooms (AAORs). Following the 1974 reorganisation of local governments this bunker was transferred to West Midlands Council and was demolished in 2000. The Warwickshire County Main bunker was moved to Rugby with a standby bunker at Stratford District Council's offices.

The following are examples of government and local authority Cold War bunkers associated with Warwickshire. Since the 1974 boundary changes, Shirley and Solihull are both within the West Midlands Metropolitan County.

CW05 Shirley Regional War Room bunker (NGR: SP12-77-)

The Regional War Room (RWR) for Region 9 Midlands was located at Stratford Road, Shirley, Birmingham, and was the last RWR constructed during the 1952–1956 building programme. The building was a standard RWR design consisting of a two-storey above ground reinforced concrete structure with no windows. The external walls and the roof were each approximately 1.5m (5ft) thick. The main room located in the centre of the bunker was the two-storey operations/map room. Surrounding the operations/map room on the ground floor and first floors were rooms for the Regional Commissioner, regional officers, civil defence staff, fire, police, military officers, medical staff, despatch riders, telephonists, dormitories, welfare facilities and plant rooms for telephone equipment, ventilation equipment, a standby generator and electrical equipment.

Shirley RWR became redundant when the Regional Seat of Government facility at Drakelow reached operational status. Eventually, the Shirley RWR bunker was bought by British Gas/Transco and used mainly for archive storage. The site was sold for redevelopment and during June 2005 the Shirley RWR bunker was demolished.

CW06 Rugby County Main Emergency Centre bunker (NGR: SP 502756)

The Rugby County Main bunker was located in The Retreat council building at Newbold Road, Rugby. It was the County Main bunker for Warwickshire from 1974 until the end of the Cold War.

CW07 Stratford Emergency Centre bunker (NGR: SP 200547)

The Stratford emergency centre bunker was located in the Stratford District Council offices building Church Street, Stratford-upon-Avon. The bunker was a standby facility for the Rugby County Main bunker.

CW08 Warwickshire County Emergency Centre bunker (NGR: SP 281651)

The Warwickshire County Emergency Centre bunker was constructed in 1966 to replace a civil defence control centre located in Warwick. The emergency centre is located in the sub-basement of the Shire Hall, Barrack Street, Warwick. The facility was upgraded in 1985 and is still operational and available to deal with emergencies that may occur in the county.

Principal rooms within the facility include:

> Agency room (for fire, ambulance and police emergency representatives)
> Manager's room
> Operations room
> Press room
> Communications room
> Radio room
> Kitchen and toilet
> Ventilation plant room
> Generator room

Entrance to the facility is via an air lock lobby fitted with gas tight doors. The facility is provided with two emergency escape routes, one via a cat ladder in a vertical shaft to the roof, and one via a tunnel to the nearby multi-storey car park. Both escape routes are fitted with gas-tight doors.

CW09 Solihull County Emergency Centre bunker (NGR: SP 149796)

Solihull County Emergency Centre bunker was located in the basement of The Council House, Homer Road, Solihull. The bunker was opened in 1967, refurbished in 1989 and remained operational until the end of the Cold War. The principal facilities were a control room, communications centre, offices, kitchen, toilets, ventilation plant room, tank room and an external emergency generator. Emergency planning facilities are now located in offices elsewhere and the bunker rooms are mainly used for storage purposes.

Radar and Telecommunications

Radar

Following the end of the Second World War the national radar installations went into decline. However, with the onset of the Cold War a programme code named Rotor was launched to upgrade UK air defences. Rotor resulted in huge expenditure in building new radar installations and new protected operations rooms. Eastern region operations rooms were generally underground bunkers and the western region operations rooms were protected surface bunkers or semi-underground bunkers. In addition, sector command and control underground bunkers were built and extremely well protected to ensure their operational effectiveness. Anti-Aircraft Operations Rooms (AAORs) were built to control the AA guns in gun-defended areas.

Within Warwickshire AAORs were constructed to control the AA guns serving the Coventry/Rugby and Birmingham gun-defended areas. The Coventry/Rugby AAOR (CW10) was located in Stoneleigh Deer Park, south of Coventry and the Birmingham AAOR (CW11) was located at Wylde Green, near Sutton Coldfield. The bunkers at both locations have been demolished. As mentioned in a previous section of this book the Wylde Green AAOR was utilised up to 1974 as Warwickshire's protected emergency headquarters bunker.

CW12 Rugby Radio Station (NGR: SP 554746)

The Rugby Radio Station, located near Hillmorton to the east of Rugby, was operational from January 1926. At the time of opening, the station's transmitter was the most powerful in the world, capable of global transmissions. Defence-related transmissions included very low frequency radio communications with ships and submarines. During the Second World War signals were transmitted to confuse and jam German aircraft radio control frequencies and technology moved on to such an extent that during the Cold War period there was speculation that Rugby Radio Station was the contact point for communication with Britain's nuclear submarines. Peter Hennessey, in his book *The Secret State*, writes that the purpose was to relay the Prime Minister's instructions to commanders of the deterrent-bearing submarines.

The Rugby Radio Station's current main function is to transmit accurate time signals derived from the National Physical Laboratory atomic clock. The BT contract for this work expires in 2007, and thus the future of the station and its masts is somewhat uncertain.

Telecommunications

Within the context of any armed conflict, reliable telecommunications installations are vital for the defence and effective governance of the country involved. During the Second World War above ground telephone installations in populated areas were particularly susceptible to disruption from bombing. With the onset of the Cold War, telecommunications were also vulnerable to destruction by electromagnetic pulse (EMP) from nuclear airburst explosions. Projects were established in the 1950s to improve the protection of telecommunications by building hardened underground emergency Telephone Trunk Exchanges (TTEs), and to route landlines deep underground. The original plan was to build main trunk cable routes between underground TTEs in London, Birmingham, Manchester, Glasgow and Bristol, and eight intermediate protected Carrier Repeater Stations (CREs). The original plan was downgraded and TTEs were only constructed in London (Kingsway), Birmingham (Anchor) and Manchester (Guardian). The installations were complete by 1958, but soon became obsolete, mainly due to the vulnerability of the main trunk lines. From the mid-1950s a microwave transmissions system was developed for national defence and civilian use, and came to be known as Backbone. Backbone consisted of a network of radio stations and microwave towers across Britain, intended to be operational should landlines sustain serious damage. The Backbone towers were designed to withstand nuclear blast waves and were generally built well away from areas that were high risk targets. From terminal stations at the towers were communication links to military establishments, emergency centres and local exchanges.

CW12 Rugby Radio Station main transmitter building and 250m-high (820ft) masts viewed from the A5 Trunk Road (June 2006)

Examples of telecommunications installations associated with the Cold War and Warwickshire include:

CW13 Birmingham Anchor Emergency TTE (NGR: SP065872)

Anchor was the codename for the underground Birmingham Emergency Telephone Trunk Exchange (TTE). The codename was derived from the Birmingham assay office anchor mark. The construction works for the TTE commenced in 1953 and it was opened in 1957.

The TTE is located approximately 30.5m (100ft) below Telephone House telephone exchange, Newhall Street, Birmingham. The complex consisted of two main tunnel chambers for the telephone equipment, smaller chambers for office accommodation, interconnecting tunnels and small tunnels for the outgoing telephone lines. Seven vertical shafts were constructed and the main access was via lift shafts located in buildings in Newhall Street, Lionel Street and Church Street. At the bottom of the lifts were heavyweight blast entrance doors. The TEE was provided with three emergency generators and air conditioning that maintained a positive air pressure to prevent the ingress of contaminates.

The TTE was maintained until the late 1980s, but is now decommissioned with the tunnels only used for cable routes. Within the tunnels pumps operate to remove the excess water ingress caused by a rise in the water table due to the reduction in water usage by industry,.

Protected Carrier Repeater Stations (CRSs) local to the Birmingham TTE were Queslett CRE, north-west of Birmingham, and Lyndon Green CRE, south-east of Birmingham. The main purpose of the CRSs was to amplify the telephone signals at intervals in the trunk lines. The buildings were designed to be blast-proof.

CW14 Birmingham BT Tower (NGR: SP 066873)

Birmingham BT Tower is located in Lionel Street and was completed in 1969. The height of the tower is 152m (500ft). The concrete core of the tower was designed to withstand the blast from a 1 megaton nuclear bomb detonated as close as 1 mile from the tower. The tower links with the Backbone network but is not in the Backbone primary chain of towers that are located in areas remote from major city centres. The nearest Backbone primary microwave tower is located north at Pye Green, Cannock, Staffordshire.

CW15 Charwelton BT Tower (NGR: SP 513563)

Charwelton BT Tower is not located in Warwickshire, but is a conspicuous landmark viewed from the south-east of the county. The tower is located 1.5 miles west of Charwelton in Northamptonshire and 300m from the Warwickshire county boundary and was built of reinforced concrete in the mid-1960s as part of the Backbone microwave communications network. The height of the tower is 118m (388ft). The design preference for Backbone towers was steel construction but in a number of locations concrete towers were more visually acceptable to the Royal Fine Arts Commission and environmental groups.

The Backbone primary towers to the north and south of Charwelton are Coalville (Leicestershire) and Stokenchurch (Buckinghamshire) respectively.

CW15 Charwelton BT Tower, Northamptonshire (July 2006).

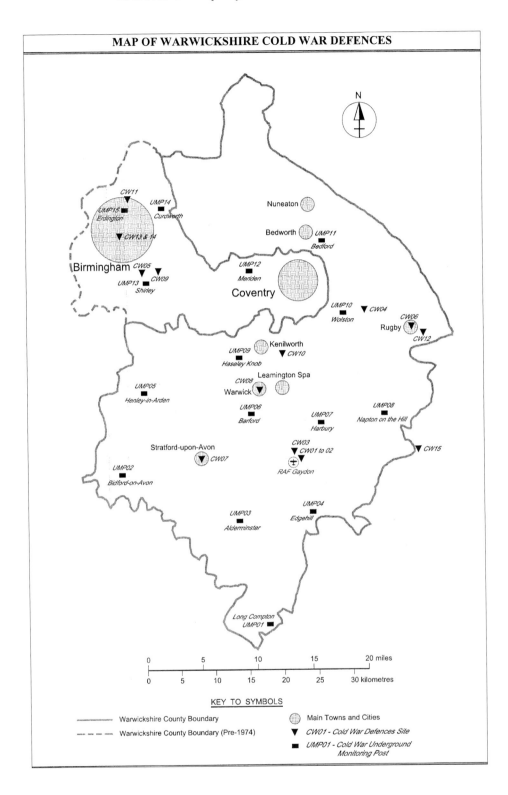

MAP OF WARWICKSHIRE COLD WAR DEFENCES

N

CW11
UMP14
Curdworth
UMP15
Erdington
Nuneaton
Bedworth
UMP11
Bedford
CW13 & 14
Birmingham CW05
UMP12
CW09
Meriden
Coventry
UMP13
Shirley
UMP10
CW04
Wolston
CW06
Rugby
CW12
Kenilworth
UMP09
CW10
Haseley Knob
Leamington Spa
UMP05
CW08
Warwick
Henley-in-Arden
UMP06
UMP07
UMP08
Barford
Harbury
Napton on the Hill
CW03
Stratford-upon-Avon
CW01 to 02
CW15
UMP02
CW07
Bidford-on-Avon
RAF Gaydon
UMP04
UMP03
Edgehill
Alderminster

Long Compton
UMP01

| 0 | 5 | 10 | 15 | 20 miles |
| 0 | 5 | 10 | 15 | 20 | 25 | 30 kilometres |

KEY TO SYMBOLS

Warwickshire County Boundary   Main Towns and Cities

Warwickshire County Boundary (Pre-1974)   ▼ *CW01 - Cold War Defences Site*

■ *UMP01 - Cold War Underground Monitoring Post*

Appendix 1

Warwickshire Pillbox Types

Summary of Warwickshire pillbox types with reference codes for locations of the pillboxes.
Refer to Appendix 2: Warwickshire Defences Gazetteer for national grid reference locations for individual pillboxes.

PILLBOX TYPE, PLAN AND REFERENCE CODES 0 1 2 3 4 5 metres	PILLBOX MAIN FEATURES
TYPE 22 **PB05, PB06 and PB09**	Regular hexagon in plan. Space for six men armed with five light machine guns (LMGs) and one rifle. Five LMG embrasures and one rifle embrasure adjacent to the single entrance. Construction generally brickwork inner and outer walls to form shuttering for reinforced concrete infill.
TYPE 22 (VARIANT) **PB38**	Regular hexagon in plan. Space for six men armed with six light machine guns. Six LMG embrasures and two entrances. Reinforced concrete construction throughout with three concrete panel anti-ricochet walls radiating from a central concrete circular column.
TYPE 24 **PB07, PB36, PB37 and PB39**	Irregular hexagon in plan with the wall containing the entrance longer than the other walls. Space for seven men armed with five light machine guns and two rifles. Five LMG embrasures and two rifle embrasures either side of the entrance. Construction generally brickwork inner and outer walls to form shuttering for reinforced concrete infill (PB07) or concrete throughout. (PB36, PB37 and PB39)

PILLBOX TYPE, PLAN AND REFERENCE CODES	PILLBOX MAIN FEATURES
STENT **PB01 to PB04 and PB21**	Square in plan. Space for five men armed with four light machine guns and one rifle. Stent pillboxes are prefabricated type with precast concrete inner and outer panels secured between vertical posts to form shuttering for reinforced concrete infill.
MUSHROOM **PB31, PB32 and PB33**	Circular in plan. Space for eight men armed with light machine guns. Embrasure with a 360-degree continuous unrestricted view. Two entrances via sunken holes. Continuous steel tubular rail below embrasure for LMG mount. Brickwork inner and outer walls to form shuttering for reinforced concrete infill. Reinforced concrete circular roof supported by cruciform brickwork walls.
RAF VARIANT **PB38 to PB58**	Rectangular in plan. Space for eight men armed with light machine guns. Generally eight embrasures with one in each face and one in each corner. One entrance below one corner embrasure. Construction is solid brickwork walls and reinforced concrete roof.

Appendix 2

Warwickshire Defences Gazetteer

WARWICKSHIRE STOP LINE PILLBOXES				
REF.	**TYPE**	**GRID**	**LOCATION**	**CONDITION (2006)**
PILLBOXES ON THE SOUTHERN COMMAND OXFORD CANAL STOP LINE (Claydon to Warwick)				
PB01	Stent	SP 458548	Oxford Canal, WNW of Stoneton Moat Farm, near Priors Hardwick.	Fair
PB02	Stent	SP 462565	Oxford Canal, bridge 122, near Priors Hardwick.	Fair
PB03	Stent	SP 459596	Oxford Canal, bridge 116, Holt Farm, near Napton-on-the-Hill.	Good
PB04	Stent	SP 458603	Oxford Canal, Lock No.10, near Napton-on-the-Hill.	Good
PB05	FW3/22	SP 433648	Grand Union Canal, near Stockton.	Destroyed
PB06	FW3/22	SP 381639	Grand Union Canal (south side), Longhole bridge, near Bascote.	Destroyed
PB07	FW3/24	SP 353649	Grand Union Canal, near Radford Semele.	Good
PB08	Not known	SP 339649	Grand Union Canal, near Radford Semele.	Destroyed
PILLBOXES ON THE WESTERN COMMAND AVON STOP LINE (Bidford-on-Avon to Coventry)				
PB09	FW3/22	SP 298654	Railway viaduct over the river Avon, Warwick.	Destroyed
PB10	Not known	SP 267610	River Avon, Barford Bridge, Sherbourne.	Destroyed
PILLBOXES ON THE WESTERN COMMAND NAPTON TO COVENTRY STOP LINE				
PB21	Stent	SP 523758	Oxford Canal, bridge 66, Clifton on Dunsmore.	Good

PILLBOXES ON THE WESTERN COMMAND COVENTRY TO TAMWORTH STOP LINE				
REF.	**TYPE**	**GRID**	**LOCATION**	**CONDITION (2006)**
PB25	Conversion	SK 251043	Coventry Canal at Alvecote Priory near Polesworth.	Good
COVENTRY ANTI-TANK ISLAND PILLBOX				
PB28	Variant	SP 319835	Coventry to Keresley minor road, opposite Manor Farm. (WM)	Good

WARWICKSHIRE ANTI-TANK BLOCKS				
ATB01	Octagonal (2)	SP 459594	Oxford Canal, bridge 116, near Napton-on-the-Hill.	Fair
ATB02	Octagonal (2)	SP 457604	Oxford Canal, bridge 114, near Napton-on-the-Hill.	Good
ATB03	Octagonal (2)	SP 382666	Bridge over disused LM&S railway, near Offchurch.	Fair
ATB04	Octagonal (1)	SP 359651	Disused LM&S railway near Offchurch.	Good
ATB05	Polygon (2)	SP 280631	River Avon, Leafield Bridge, Lodge Wood, Warwick.	Good
ATB06	Cylinder (6)	SP 432534	Wormleighton Road near junction with the A423 (T) road.	Good
ATB07	Cylinder (20)	SP 525674	On each side of A45, Willoughby.	Good
ATB08	Cylinder (4)	SP 526653	Entrance to Wolfhamcote Hall, near Braunston.	Good
ATB09	Cylinder (2)	SP 531659	Oxford Canal, bridge 95, near Braunston.	Fair
ATB10	Pimple (10+)	SP 488773	Two groups near Oxford Canal, bridge 50, Newbold on Avon.	Good
ATB11	Cylinder (5)	SP 511778	Brownsover Lane, near Rugby.	Fair
ATB12	Vertical Rail (4)	SP 510776	Brownsover Lane, near Rugby.	Fair
ATB13	Cylinder (10)	SP 509776	Brownsover Lane, near Rugby.	Fair
ATB14	Cylinder (1)	SP 508775	Brownsover Lane, near Rugby.	Fair
ATB15	Pimple (13)	SP 503771	Old Leicester Road, Rugby. North side of road tunnel passing under the Oxford Canal.	Fair
ATB16	Cylinder (6)	SP 279905	Front garden lawn, Old Arley.	Good
ATB17	Cylinder (200+)	SP 274903	Farm house garden wall, by a road tee junction, Devitts Green, 0.5 miles west of Old Arley.	Good
ATB18	Cylinder (3) + Cube (1)	SP 260864	On grass verge in front of a factory, Green End, 1.5 miles west of Fillongley.	Fair

REF.	TYPE	GRID	LOCATION	CONDITION (2006)
ATB19	Cylinder (2)	SP 232881	On grass verge, Fillongley Road, 1 mile north of Maxstoke.	Good
ATB20	Cylinder (6)	SP 458787	Oxford Canal, bridge 37, south-west of Easenhall.	Fair
ATB21	Cylinder (8)	SP 468784	Oxford Canal, bridge 42, near Harborough Magna.	Fair
ATB22	Cube (4)	SP 277782	Tile Hill Lane and Banner Lane road junction, Coventry.	Good
ATB23	Cylinder (1)	SP 213962	By river Tame footbridge, Kingsbury.	Good

WARWICKSHIRE RAF AIRFIELD BUILDINGS

Note: The majority of the airfield buildings listed below are on private land with no public access.

REF.	TYPE	GRID	LOCATION	RAF AIRFIELD	CONDITION (2006)
AB01	C1 hangars (2)	SP 409882 SP 407881	Within Gamecock Army Barracks, Wolvey.	Bramcote	Fair
AB02	J hangar	SP 267546	Within industrial estate.	Wellesbourne Mountford	Good
AB03	T1 hangars (4)	SP 269547	Within industrial estate.	Wellesbourne Mountford	Good
AB04	Bellman hangars (4)	SP 349745	Within Coventry Airport.	Baginton	Good
AB05	Bellman hangars	SP 452743	Within industrial estate.	Church Lawford	Fair
AB06	T2 hangars (3)	SP 350747	Within Coventry Airport.	Baginton	Good
AB07	Hangars (2)	SP 334612	Adjacent to Harbury Lane, south of Leamington Spa.	Leamington Spa	Fair
AB08	B1 hangar	SP 211512	Within industrial estate. No public access.	Stratford	Fair
AB09	Control tower	SP 409881	Within Gamecock Army Barracks, Wolvey.	Bramcote	Good
AB10	Control tower	SP 175489	Located on airfield. Currently used by light aircraft flying club.	Long Marston	Fair
AB11	Control tower	SP 218516	Adjacent to Ailstone Farm. No public access.	Stratford	Poor
AB12	Control tower	SP 450733	Within landfill site and also sand and gravel extraction site.	Church Lawford	Poor
AB13	Guard house	SP 409885	Entrance to Gamecock Army Barracks.	Bramcote	Good
AB14	Station headquarters	SP 408886	Entrance to Gamecock Army Barracks.	Bramcote	Good
AB15	Motor transport buildings	SP 409883	Within Gamecock Army Barracks, Wolvey.	Bramcote	Good

REF.	TYPE	GRID	LOCATION	RAF AIRFIELD	CONDITION (2006)
AB16	Workshops	SP 408884	Within Gamecock Army Barracks, Wolvey.	Bramcote	Good
AB17	Admin. buildings	SP 409885	Within Gamecock Army Barracks, Wolvey.	Bramcote	Good
AB18	Water tank steel tower	SP 220506	On private farmland. Adjacent to public footpath.	Stratford	Fair
AB19	Storage shed	SP 223506	On private land. Adjacent to public footpath.	Stratford	Fair
AB20	Technical buildings	SP 224507	On private land. Adjacent to public footpath.	Stratford	Fair
AB21	Bomb store	SP 223515	On private farmland. No public access.	Stratford	Fair
AB22	Fire tender building	SP 454736	On private farmland on the north-east side of the former airfield.	Church Lawford	Poor
AB23	Shooting range	SP 412883	Within Gamecock Army Barracks, Wolvey.	Bramcote	Good
AB24	Shooting range	SP 224517	On private farmland. No public access.	Stratford	Fair
AB25	Turret trainer	SP 177487	On private farmland west of B4632 road.	Long Marston	Fair
AB26	Sergeants' mess	SP 403886	Within Gamecock Army Barracks, Wolvey.	Bramcote	Good
AB27	Officers' mess	SP 403885	Within Gamecock Army Barracks, Wolvey.	Bramcote	Good
AB28	H-block barracks (6)	SP 406884	Within Gamecock Army Barracks, Wolvey.	Bramcote	Fair
AB29	Domestic buildings	SP 181491	On private farmland east of B4632 road.	Long Marston	Poor
AB30	Domestic buildings	SP 220504	On private farmland. Adjacent to public footpath.	Stratford	Poor
AB31	Gymnasium building	SP 451727	On private farmland. Adjacent to public road.	Church Lawford	Poor
AB32	Gymnasium building	SP 355555	Within Land Rover design and test centre but visible from B4100 road.	Gaydon	Poor
AB33	De-contamin. building	SP 221505	On private farmland. Adjacent to public footpath.	Stratford	Poor
AB34	Nissen hut	SP 349746	Within Coventry Airport adjacent to a Bellman Hangar.	Baginton	Fair
AB35	Nissen hut	SP 179492	On private farmland east of B4632 road.	Long Marston	Poor
AB36	Romney hut	SP 182491	On private farmland east of B4632 road.	Long Marston	Fair

	WARWICKSHIRE RAF AIRFIELD PILLBOXES			
REF.	**TYPE**	**GRID**	**LOCATION**	**CONDITION (2006)**
PB31	Mushroom	SP 175494	Former RAF Long Marston, near Stratford-upon-Avon.	Good
PB32	Mushroom	SP 176494	Former RAF Long Marston, near Stratford-upon-Avon.	Good
PB33	Mushroom	SP 175493	Former RAF Long Marston, near Stratford-upon-Avon.	Good
PB34	Not known	SP 170496	Former RAF Long Marston, near Stratford-upon-Avon.	Destroyed
PB35	Not known	SP 170488	Former RAF Long Marston, near Stratford-upon-Avon.	Destroyed
PB36	FW3/24	SP 219513	Former RAF Stratford (Atherstone).	Good
PB37	FW3/24	SP 212520	Former RAF Stratford (Atherstone).	Good
PB38	FW3/22 (Variant)	SP 454729	Former RAF Church Lawford (beside road on east edge of former airfield).	Good
PB39	FW3/24	SP 458735	Former RAF Church Lawford (Lawford Heath Lane).	Destroyed
PB40	RAF Variant	SP 417876	Former RAF Bramcote, near Wolvey (on high ground covering south-east approaches).	Fair
PB41	RAF Variant	SP 418875	Former RAF Bramcote, near Wolvey (corner of B4109 and minor road).	Fair
PB42	RAF Variant	SP 405869	Former RAF Bramcote, near Wolvey (corner of B4109 and airfield track).	Fair
PB43	RAF Variant	SP 403879	Former RAF Bramcote, near Wolvey.	Destroyed
PB44	RAF Variant	SP 404889	Former RAF Bramcote, near Wolvey.	Destroyed
PB45	RAF Variant	SP 408887	Former RAF Bramcote, near Wolvey.	Destroyed
PB46	RAF Variant	SP 410885	Former RAF Bramcote, near Wolvey.	Destroyed
PB47	RAF Variant	SP 404883	Former RAF Bramcote, near Wolvey.	Destroyed
PB48	RAF Variant	SP 406881	Former RAF Bramcote, near Wolvey.	Destroyed
PB49	RAF Variant	SP 407881	Former RAF Bramcote, near Wolvey.	Destroyed
PB50	RAF Variant	SP 408880	Former RAF Bramcote, near Wolvey.	Destroyed
PB51	RAF Variant	SP 412882	Former RAF Bramcote, near Wolvey.	Destroyed
PB52	RAF Variant	SP 405872	Former RAF Bramcote, near Wolvey.	Destroyed

REF.	TYPE	GRID	LOCATION	CONDITION (2006)
PB53	RAF Variant	SP 404873	Former RAF Bramcote, near Wolvey.	Destroyed
PB54	RAF Variant	SP 414883	Former RAF Bramcote, near Wolvey.	Destroyed
PB55	RAF Variant	SP 416881	Former RAF Bramcote, near Wolvey.	Destroyed
PB56	RAF Variant	SP 415873	Former RAF Bramcote, near Wolvey.	Destroyed
PB57	RAF Variant	SP 415870	Former RAF Bramcote, near Wolvey.	Destroyed
PB58	RAF Variant	SP 405874	Former RAF Bramcote, near Wolvey.	Fair
PB59	Not known	SP 348746	Former RAF Baginton, near Coventry.	Destroyed
PB60	Not known	SP 349747	Former RAF Baginton, near Coventry.	Destroyed
PB61	FW3/24	SP 163838	Former RAF Elmdon (West Midlands).	Destroyed

WARWICKSHIRE RAF AIRFIELD BATTLE HEADQUARTERS				
BH01	11008/41	SP 175494	Former RAF Long Marston, near Stratford-upon-Avon.	Fair
BH02	11008/41	SP 211520	Former RAF Stratford (Atherstone).	Fair
BH03	11008/41	SP 265545	Former RAF Wellesbourne Mountford.	Restored
BH04	11008/41	SP 344741	Former RAF Baginton, near Coventry (remote from airfield perimeter).	Good
BH05	Not known	SP 415872	Former RAF Bramcote, near Wolvey.	Destroyed
BH06	11008/41	SP 164836	Former RAF Elmdon, by A45 road, Birmingham Airport (West Midlands).	Fair

WARWICKSHIRE ANTI-AIRCRAFT DEFENCES				
AA01	Searchlight battery	SP 32-50-	Four ring ditches crop marks, 0.5 miles north-east of Butlers Marston.	Crop marks
AA02	Searchlight battery	SP 25-54-	Three ring ditches crop marks, 1 mile south-west of Wellesbourne.	Crop marks
AA03	Searchlight battery	SP 31-59-	Four ring ditches crop marks, east of Tollgate Farm, and 1 mile south of Bishop's Tachbrook.	Crop marks
AA04	LAA battery	SP 39-62-	Ring ditches crop marks, Frizmore Hill, near Pounce Hill Farm, 1.5 miles south of Radford Semele.	Crop marks

REF.	TYPE	GRID	LOCATION	CONDITION (2006)
AA05	LAA battery	SP 16-69-	Ring ditches crop marks, 0.5 miles north-west of Copt Green, near Lapworth.	Crop marks
AA06	HAA battery (-) (H11)	SP 130719	Nuthurst HAA, 1 mile west of Nuthurst, near Hockley Heath (Birmingham GDA).	Destroyed
AA07	HAA battery (-) (H25)	SP 275693	Bannerhill HAA, adjacent to farm road/footpath, near Goodrest Farm, Rouncil Lane, Kenilworth (Coventry GDA).	Good
AA08	LAA batteries	Various	Various LAA sites built to protect Leamington Spa.	Destroyed
AA09	HAA battery (-) (H28)	SP 329736	Stoneleigh HAA, near B4115 road south-west of Finham Bridge, near Stoneleigh (Coventry GDA).	Destroyed
AA10	Searchlight battery	SP 398645	Three ring ditches crop marks, 0.75s miles south-east of Long Itchington. Searchlight carriage SP 397644.	Crop marks
AA11	LAA battery	SP 45-72-	Three ring ditches crop marks, 0.5 miles south of Lawford Heath, near the A45 trunk road.	Crop marks
AA12	LAA batteries	Various	Various LAA sites built to protect Rugby. See Warwickshire County Council website.	Poor
AA13	LAA battery	SP 39-84-	Four ring ditches crop marks, 0.5 miles east of Barnacle, south of Bulkington.	Crop marks
AA14	HAA battery (-) (H27)	SP 301871	Fillongley HAA, near High House Farm, Breach Oak Lane, 1 mile east of Fillongley (Coventry GDA).	Fair
AA15	Searchlight battery	SP 24-95-	Ring ditches crop marks, south of Hurley, 0.5 miles north-east of Foul End, east of Kingsbury.	Destroyed
AA16	HAA battery (A) (H2)	SP 378865	Bedworth HAA. 1 mile east of Bedworth (Coventry GDA).	Destroyed
AA17	HAA battery (B) (H71)	SP 382833	Brookfield Farm HAA, 1 mile north-east of Potter's Green (Coventry GDA).	Destroyed
AA18	HAA battery (C) (H23)	SP 378779	Binley HAA, 3 miles east of Coventry (Coventry GDA).	Destroyed
AA19	HAA battery (D) (H30)	SP 382741	Ryton on Dunsmore HAA, 200m south-west of Ryton on Dunsmore (Coventry GDA.	Destroyed
AA20	HAA battery (E) (-)	SP 356728	Bubbenhall (a) HAA, 0.75 mile north-west of Bubbenhall (Coventry GDA).	Destroyed
AA21	HAA battery (F) (H67)	SP 304751	Gibbet Hill HAA, 200m west of Gibbet Hill Road, Coventry (Coventry GDA).	Destroyed
AA22	HAA battery (G) (H26)	SP 284781	Tile Hill HAA, 3 miles west of Coventry (Coventry GDA).	Destroyed
AA23	HAA battery (H) (H72)	SP 318801	Keresley HAA, 3 miles north-west of Coventry (Coventry GDA).	Destroyed
AA24	HAA battery (K) (H68)	SP 340804	Exhall HAA, 3 miles north of Coventry (Coventry GDA).	Destroyed
AA25	HAA battery (L) (H69)	SP 382801	Walsgrave HAA, 3 miles east of Coventry (Coventry GDA).	Destroyed

REF.	TYPE	GRID	LOCATION	CONDITION (2006)
AA26	HAA battery (-) (H22)	SP 433897	Wolvey HAA, 1 mile north of Wolvey (Coventry GDA).	Destroyed
AA27	HAA battery (-) (H24)	SP 406658	Long Itchington HAA, 0.5 miles north-west of Long Itchington (Coventry GDA).	Destroyed
AA28	HAA battery (-) (H29)	SP 472785	Cathiron HAA, 0.75 miles south-west of Harborough Magna (Coventry GDA).	Destroyed
AA29	HAA battery (-) (H66)	SP 343714	Bubbenhall (b) HAA, 0.75 miles east of Stareton (Coventry GDA).	Destroyed
AA30	HAA battery (-) (H70)	SP 292798	Eastern Green HAA, 3 miles west of Coventry (Coventry GDA).	Destroyed

Note: HAA battery (A) denotes the pre-1942 Coventry GDA site code and (H2) denotes the post-1942 site code following the amalgamation of the Coventry GDA and Birmingham GDA.

WARWICKSHIRE BOMBING DECOY SITES				
REF.	TYPE	GRID	DECOY SITE NAME AND LOCATION	CONDITION (2006)
BD01	Q site	SP 309480	Pillerton Priors – decoy for RAF Wellesbourne. Decoy site located 1 mile north-east of Pillerton Priors. Generator building at NGR: SP 309476.	Fair – generator building
BD02	Q site	SP 218616	Wolverton – decoy for RAF Honiley. Decoy site located south-east of Wolverton.	Destroyed
BD03	Q site	SP 129611	Wootton Wawen – decoy for RAF Honiley. Decoy site located, 2 miles south-west of Wootton Wawen.	Destroyed
BD04	SF, QF and QL site	SP 364676	Hunningham – decoy for Coventry. Decoy site located 1 mile south-west of Hunningham. Control shelter building at NGR: SP 364672.	Fair – control shelter
BD05	QL site	SP 395680	Eathorpe – decoy for Coventry. Decoy site located 0.75 miles south of Eathorpe.	Destroyed
BD06	SF, QL and M site	SP 450680	Leamington Hastings – decoy for Coventry and Armstong Whitworth factory, Baginton. Decoy site located 0.5 miles north-east of Leamington Hastings. Control shelter building at NGR: SP 463674.	Poor – control shelter
BD07	QF and QL site	SP 358706	Bubbenhall – decoy for Coventry. Decoy site located 1 mile south of Bubbenhall.	Destroyed
BD08	SF site	SP 418777	Bretford – decoy for Coventry. Decoy site located 0.75 miles west of Bretford. Control shelter building at NGR: SP 414769.	Fair – control shelter
BD09	QF and QL site	SP 272829	Meriden – decoy for Coventry. Decoy site located 1.5 miles NE of Meriden. Control shelter building at NGR: SP 275833.	Good – control shelter
BD10	QL site	Not traced	Astley – decoy for Coventry. Location not traced.	Destroyed

REF.	TYPE	GRID	DECOY SITE NAME AND LOCATION	CONDITION (2006)
BD11	Q site	SP 472864	Wibtoft – decoy for RAF Bramcote. Decoy site located 1 mile south of Wibtoft. Control shelter building at NGR: SP 468864.	Fair – control shelter
BD12	SF and QL site	SP 536712	Barby – decoy for Rugby. Decoy site located 3 miles south-east of Rugby, within Northamptonshire.	Destroyed
BD13	SF site	SP 600783	Clay Coton – decoy for Rugby. Decoy site located 6.5 miles east of Rugby, within Northamptonshire.	Destroyed
BD14	QL site	Not traced	Shenton – decoy for Nuneaton. Location not traced.	Destroyed
BD15	SF site	SP 283453	Halford – decoy for Birmingham. Decoy site located 1.5 miles east of Halford.	Destroyed
BD16	SF and QL site	SP 103646	Moreton Bagot - decoy for Birmingham and Redditch. Decoy site located 0.75 miles west of Moreton Bagot.	Destroyed
BD17	QF and QL site	SP 107674	Mappleborough – decoy for Birmingham. Decoy site located 1 mile west of Ullenhall.	Destroyed
BD18	SF and Q site	SP 224868	Maxstoke – decoy for Birmingham. Decoy site located 1 mile west of Maxstoke.	Destroyed
BD19	QF and QL site	SP 228966	Kingsbury – decoy for Birmingham. Decoy site located 1 mile east of Kingsbury.	Destroyed
BD20	SF site	SP 213768	Balsall – decoy for Birmingham. Decoy site located 2 miles west of Balsall Common, within West Midlands.	Destroyed
BD21	SF and QL site	SP 180816	Bickenhill – decoy for Birmingham. Decoy site located 1 mile south-west of Bickenhill, within West Midlands.	Destroyed
BD22	QF and QL site	SP 162936	Overgreen – decoy for Birmingham. Decoy site located 1 mile north-west of Curdworth, within West Midlands.	Destroyed

WARWICKSHIRE AIR-RAID SHELTERS				
REF.	TYPE	GRID	LOCATION	CONDITION (2006)
AR01	Stanton	SP 425613	0.75 miles south-east of Southam, in allotments adjacent to the Welsh Road to Priors Marston.	Good
AR02	Domestic	SP 531764	West side of Church Street, Clifton upon Dunsmore.	Good
AR03	Domestic	SP 528762	Opposite village school, in South Road, Clifton upon Dunsmore.	Good
AR04	Various	Various	Various locations in Kenilworth (see main text).	Fair
AR05	Stanton	SP 55-26-	North-east perimeter of former RAF Wellesbourne Mountford Airfield.	Destroyed
AR06	Stanton	SP 211512	Near A3400 road, by the west perimeter of former RAF Stratford (Atherstone).	Poor

REF.	TYPE	GRID	LOCATION	CONDITION (2006)
AR07	Blast shelter	SP 218515	Near Ailstone Farm, within former RAF Stratford (Atherstone).	Poor
AR08	Stanton	SP 218522	Near the northern perimeter of former RAF Stratford (Atherstone).	Fair
AR09	Stanton	SP 176492	Long Marston Airfield, near Stratford-upon-Avon.	Fair
AR10	Stanton	SP 180492	Long Marston Airfield, dispersed site near Stratford-upon-Avon.	Good

WARWICKSHIRE ARMY BARRACKS AND DEPOTS

REF.	TYPE	GRID	NAME AND LOCATION	CONDITION (2006)
ABD01	Barracks	SP 258649	Budbrooke Barracks, 1.5 miles west of Warwick (demolished 1960).	Demolished
ABD02	Barracks	SP 405885	Gamecock Barracks, Bramcote, 3 miles south-east of Nuneaton (active MoD army barracks). No public access.	Good
ABD03	Depot and Barracks	SP 375515	Kineton Depot, 3.5 miles east of Kineton (active MoD depot). No public access.	Good
ABD04	Depot and Barracks	SP 160470	Long Marston Depot, 5 miles south-east of Stratford-upon-Avon (MoD depot closed. Private sector storage). No public access.	Good
ABD05	Billet	SP 285524	Walton Hall, 2 miles south of Wellesbourne. (Billet for Czechoslovak Brigade 1940/42.)	Good
ABD06	Billet	SP 302556	Moreton Hall, 2 miles east of Wellesbourne. (Billet for Czechoslovak Brigade 1940/42.)	Good
ABD07	Billet	SP 305544	Moreton Paddox, 2 miles east of Wellesbourne. (Billet for Czechoslovak Brigade 1940/42.)	Demolished

WARWICKSHIRE DRILL HALLS AND TERRITORIAL ARMY CENTRES

DH01	Army	SP 197543	TA Centre, New Broad Street, Stratford-upon-Avon.	Good
DH02	Army	SP 289653	Drill Hall, Coten End, Warwick. (Currently a youth centre.)	Good
DH03	Army	SP 314657	Drill Hall, Adelaide Road, Leamington Spa. (Currently a club.)	Good
DH04	Army	SP 502758	Drill Hall, Lancaster Road, Rugby.	Demolished
DH05	Army	SP 497756	TA Centre, Seabroke House, Edward Street, Rugby.	Good
DH06	Army	SP 331787	Drill Hall, Greyfriars Road, Coventry (West Midlands).	Demolished

REF.	TYPE	GRID	NAME AND LOCATION	CONDITION (2006)
DH07	Army	SP 307777	TA Centre, Sir Henry Parkes Road, Canley, Coventry (West Midlands).	Good
DH08	Army	SP 328802	TA Centre, Westfield House, Radford Road, Coventry (West Midlands).	Good
DH09	Army	SP 070863	Drill Hall, Thorp Street, Birmingham (West Midlands).	Demolished
DH10	Army	SP 096845	TA Centre, Golden Hillock Road, Sparkbrook, Birmingham (West Midlands).	Good

WARWICKSHIRE PRISONER OF WAR CAMPS					
REF.	TYPE	GRID	PoW CAMP NAME AND LOCATION	Camp No.	CONDITION (2006)
PW01	Not known	SP 15-48-	Long Marston Camp – located by the former Royal Engineers' Depot, 6 miles south-west of Stratford-upon-Avon.	6	Demolished
PW02	Not known	SP 319672	Cloister Croft Camp – located south of Cloister Croft road, north of Leamington Spa.	25	Demolished
PW03	German working camp	SP 249476	Ettington Park Camp – located 1 mile north of Newbold-on-Stour.	31	Demolished
PW04	German working camp	SP 228889	Castle Camp – located 2 miles east of Coleshill, adjacent to Maxstoke Castle. Site now a golf course.	39	Demolished
PW05	German working camp	SP 430698	Birdingbury – located 0.5 miles south-east of Frankton adjacent to the minor road between Frankton and Birdingbury.	97	Demolished
PW06	German working camp	SP 27-64-	Racecourse Camp – adjacent to Warwick Racecourse; precise location not identified.	140	Demolished
PW07	Base Camp	SP 299980	Merevale Hall Camp – located 0.5 miles west of Atherstone, within grounds of Merevale Hall.	195/241	Demolished
PW08	Base Camp	SP 334894	Arbury Hall – located 2 miles south-west of Nuneaton, within grounds of Arbury Hall.	196	Demolished

REF.	TYPE	GRID	PoW CAMP NAME AND LOCATION	Camp No.	CONDITION (2006)
PW09	Not known	Not known	Stratford upon Avon – location not known.	233	Demolished
PW10	Not known	SP 37-51-	Marlborough Farm Camp – located 2.5 miles east of Kineton within existing Army Depot. Precise location not known.	579	Demolished
PW11	German working company	SP 343718	Stoneleigh Camp – located 1.5 miles south-east of Stoneleigh adjacent to former Second World War military hospital.	667/667a	Demolished
PW12	German working company	SP 160470	No.3 Camp Long Marston – located in the grounds of the former Royal Engineers' Depot, 6 miles south-west of Stratford-upon-Avon.	685	Demolished
PW13	German working company	SP 54-70-	Barby Camp – located near Barby, 4 miles south-east of Rugby. Precise location not known.	1005	Demolished
PW14	Not known	SP 274695	Bannerhill Camp – located Rouncil Lane, 1.5 miles south-west of Kenilworth. Huts originally used for the adjacent HAA battery crew.	Not known	Demolished
PW15	German and Italian working camp	SP 421586	Ladbroke Camp – located Radbourne Lane, Ladbroke, 2.5 miles south of Southam. One MoW concrete hut and two Nissen huts survive.	Not known	Fair

Reference: Majority of above information derived from *Prisoner of War Camps (1939–1948)* by R.J.C.Thomas © EH 2003. The Camp Number is the official number allocated to the camp during the Second World War.

WARWICKSHIRE COLD WAR DEFENCES					
REF.	TYPE	GRID	COLD WAR SITE NAME AND LOCATION	OPENED/ CLOSED	CONDITION (2006)
CW01	V-bomber hangars (2)	SP 352549	RAF Gaydon – located in Land Rover design and test centre.	1955/1974	Good
CW02	Control tower	SP 348543	RAF Gaydon – located in Land Rover design and test centre.	1955/1974	Good
CW03	Atomic bomb store	SP 319544	RAF Gaydon – located by Lighthorne Rough, west of the former airfield.	1955/1974	Fair

REF.	TYPE	GRID	COLD WAR SITE NAME AND LOCATION	OPENED/ CLOSED	CONDITION (2006)
CW04	ROC group headquarters	SP 457736	Lawford Heath (Group No.8 Coventry) – located adjacent to former RAF Church Lawford, near Rugby.	1963/1992	New usage
CW05	Regional war room bunker	SP 12-77-	Shirley War Room Region 9 – located Stratford Road, Shirley, south of Birmingham (West Midlands).	1956/60s	Destroyed 2005
CW06	Emergency County Main	SP 502756	Rugby County Main – located in The Retreat council building, Newbold Road, Rugby.	1970s/-	Not known
CW07	Emergency centre bunker	SP 200547	Stratford Emergency Centre – located Church Street, Stratford-upon-Avon.	1970s/-	Not known
CW08	Emergency centre bunker	SP 281651	Warwickshire County Emergency Centre – located in sub-basement of Shire Hall, Warwick.	1966/open	Good
CW09	Emergency centre bunker	SP 149796	Solihull Emergency Centre – located in basement of The Council House, Homer Road, Solihull (West Midlands).	1967/1992	New usage
CW10	AAOR bunker	SP 341720	Coventry/Rugby AAOR – located in Stoneleigh Deer Park, 4 miles south of Coventry.	1954/60s	Destroyed
CW11	AAOR bunker	SP 121948	Wylde Green AAOR – located St Bernard's Road, Wylde Green, Sutton Coldfield (West Midlands).	1954/2000	Destroyed
CW12	Radio station	SP 554746	Rugby Radio Station – located near Hillmorton east of Rugby.	1926/open	Good
CW13	Underground telephone exchange	SP 065872	Anchor underground Telephone Trunk Exchange. Located below Telephone House telephone exchange, Newhall Street, Birmingham (West Midlands).	1957/80s	Poor
CW14	Comms tower	SP 066873	Birmingham BT Tower – located Lionel Street, Birmingham (West Midlands).	1969/open	Good
CW15	Comms tower	SP 513563	Charwelton BT Tower – located 1.5 miles west of Charwelton (Northamptonshire).	1965/open	Good

	WARWICKSHIRE COLD WAR ROC UNDERGROUND MONITORING POSTS				
REF.	TYPE	GRID	MONITORING POST NAME AND LOCATION	OPENED/ CLOSED	CONDITION (2006)
UMP01	Cold War	SP 296310	Long Compton – located north of the Rollright Stones near to the King Stone standing stone overlooking Long Compton.	1961/1991	Destroyed
UMP02	Cold War	SP 521111	Bidford-on-Avon – located by a public footpath adjacent to the boundary fence of Bidford Grange Golf Course.	1960/1991	Fair
UMP03	Cold War	SP 252443	Alderminster – located on farmland 140m north of the minor road between Armscote and Tredington.	1963/1968	Destroyed
UMP04	Cold War	SP 374469	Edgehill – located on farmland 400m south of Edgehill, 30m west of a public footpath. Only the raised entrance hatch remains.	1963/1991	Poor
UMP05	Cold War	SP 155661	Henley-in-Arden – located adjacent to the Beaudesert motte and bailey castle.	1960/1968	Destroyed
UMP06	Cold War	SP 286599	Barford – located adjacent to private road to Wasperton Hill, 130m south of Wasperton Lane. Private land with no public access.	1959/1991	Fair (2000)
UMP07	Cold War	SP 360597	Harbury – located on farmland south-west of Harbury.	1960/1968	Destroyed
UMP08	Cold War	SP 459614	Napton-on-the-Hill – located near Napton Windmill.	1959/1968	Destroyed
UMP09	Cold War	SP 259711	Haseley Knob – located on farmland, 300m north of Rouncil Lane, 2 miles west of Kenilworth.	1964/1991	Destroyed
UMP10	Cold War	SP 419746	Wolston – located in the corner of a field at the junction of Dyer's Lane and the Fosse Way. Can be viewed from Dyer's Lane.	1960/1991	Fair

REF.	TYPE	GRID	MONITORING POST NAME AND LOCATION	OPENED/ CLOSED	CONDITION (2006)
UMP11	Cold War	SP 379856	Bedworth – located west of the B4109 Coventry Road, between Bulkington and Coventry.	1961/1991	Destroyed
UMP12	Cold War	SP 262825	Meriden – located in the corner of a field adjacent to the junction of the A45 slip road and Showell Lane, near Eaves Green (West Midlands).	1965/1991	Fair
UMP13	Cold War	SP129767	Shirley – located in the corner of a field 250m south of Dog Kennel Lane (West Midlands).	1961/1991	Destroyed
UMP14	Cold War	SP 166932	Curdworth – located 100m north of Wiggins Hill Farm, west of Curdworth (West Midlands).	1965/1968	Destroyed
UMP15	Cold War	SP 102917	Erdington – located adjacent to the south-east corner of Erdington reservoir (West Midlands).	1960/1991	Destroyed

Appendix 3

Warwickshire Second World War Defences Circular Walks

A selection of walks through the Warwickshire countryside with views of remains of Second World War defences. Each walk follows a combination of public footpaths, bridleways or canal towpaths or minor roads. **The remains of Second World War defences on the walks are all visible from public rights of way and the walker should not trespass off the walk route onto private land.** The walk route maps provide an approximate guide to the route and for more detail the walker is recommended to supplement these maps with the listed Ordnance Survey Landranger maps 151 and 140.

WALK No.	LOCATION	MILES (km)
1	Oxford Canal, Priors Hardwick	4.5 (7.2km)
2	Oxford Canal, Napton-on-the-Hill	2.5 (4km)
3	Oxford Canal, Clifton upon Dunsmore	3.5 (5.6km)
4	Grand Union Canal, Offchurch	4 (6.4km)
5	Atherstone on Stour	4.5 (7.2km)

WARWICKSHIRE WORLD WAR TWO DEFENCES

CIRCULAR WALKS

NOTATIONS FOR WALKS MAPS

- - - - - - - - - - - - - -	Walk Route
- - - - - - - - - - - -	Adjoining Footpath
▬▬▬▬▬▬▬▬▬▬	Main Road
═══════════	Minor Road
━━━━━━━━━━	Farm Track
┅┅┅┅┅┅┅┅┅	Railway
═══════════	Dismantled Railway
▬▬▬▬▬▬▬▬▬▬	Canal
────────────	River
≍	Bridge
PH	Public House
✝	Church
▨▨▨	Built-up Area
░░░	Wood
● *PB01*	WW2 Pillbox
■ *BH01*	WW2 Battle Headquarters
● *ATB01*	WW2 Anti-Tank Blocks
▲ *BD01*	WW2 Bombing Decoy Site
△ *AA01*	WW2 Anti-Aircraft Site
▢ *AR01*	WW2 Air Raid Shelter

MAP OF WALKS LOCATIONS

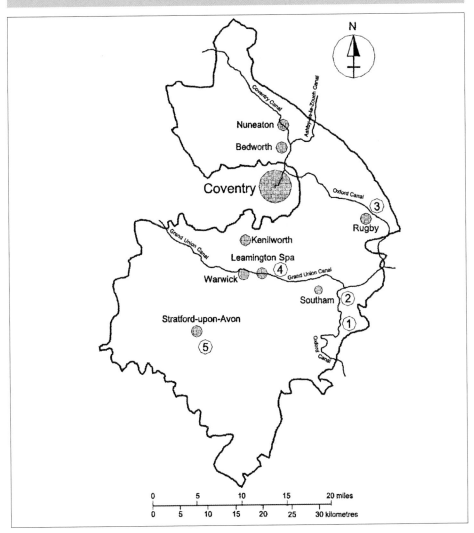

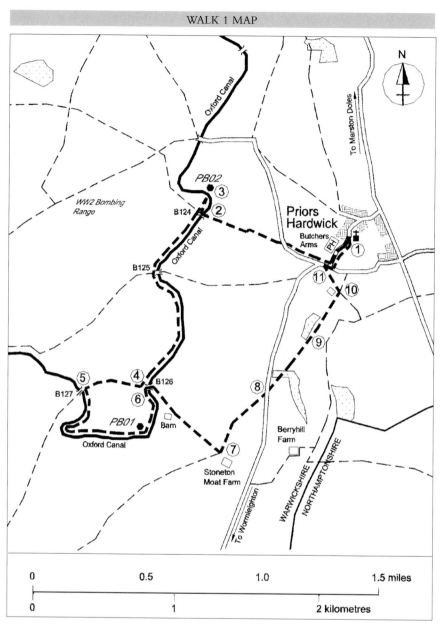

Left: PB01
Stent pillbox.

Right: PB02
Stent pillbox.

WALK 1: OXFORD CANAL, PRIORS HARDWICK	
Distance: 4.5 miles (7.2km)	**OS Map:** Landranger 151: Stratford upon Avon.

Second World War Defence Sites: Two prefabricated pillboxes PB01 and PB02 and a section of the Oxford Canal, which formed part of the Second World War Southern Command Oxford Canal Stop Line.

Directions to start: The start location is Priors Hardwick, a village 6 miles south-east of Southam. From Southam turn off the A425 to Marston Doles. Shortly after Marston Doles turn right for Priors Hardwick.

Parking: In the Priors Hardwick main street near to the church (NGR 472562). Alternatively, subject to permission, park in the car park opposite the Butchers Arms restaurant (NGR 471561).

Refreshments: The Butchers Arms restaurant, Priors Hardwick.

The Walk

Note: The walk follows public footpaths, minor roads and the Oxford Canal towpath.

1. Walk south along the village road past the Butchers Arms restaurant and right at the first road T-junction into Lower End Road. Within 50m bear right into a single-track no through road. Within 150m follow a signed footpath across fields to Oxford Canal bridge 124. *(The canal formed part of the Second World War Southern Command Oxford Canal Stop Line.)*

2. Cross bridge 124 at the Oxford Canal and turn right onto the canal towpath. Walk approximately 150m to a left-hand canal bend. *(On the opposite side of the canal towpath is Second World War pillbox PB02.)*

3. Retrace steps back to bridge 124 and continue south along the towpath past bridge 125 to arrive at bridge 126.

4. At bridge 126 turn right onto a signed footpath and follow the footpath across three fields to bridge 127.

5. At bridge 127 turn left onto the canal towpath and walk back towards bridge 126. *(At the second sharp left-hand canal bend and where overhead electric cables pass over the canal is Second World War pillbox PB01. The pillbox is adjacent to the towpath but well concealed by ivy and undergrowth.)*

6. At bridge 126 turn right and follow the footpath across fields to Stoneton Moat Farm. The farm is surrounded by an ancient water-filled moat.

7. At Stoneton Moat Farm turn left onto the farm road and follow a signed footpath across a field to a minor road.

8. Cross the road and follow a signed footpath diagonally across a field, walk through a small wood and continue to the top of a hill. From the top of the hill are fine views across the Warwickshire countryside.

9. Follow the footpath across fields along the top of the hill.

10. Turn left in the field at the first cottage and walk down hill to a gateway. Pass through the gateway and walk along the single-track road to a minor road.

11. Turn right at the minor road and within 50m turn left at the road junction and return to the start at Priors Hardwick.

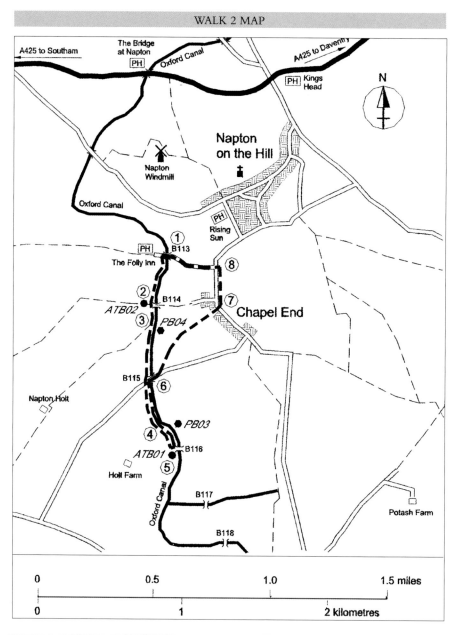

WALK 2 MAP

A425 to Southam

The Bridge at Napton
PH

Oxford Canal

AA25 to Daventry

PH Kings Head

N

Napton Windmill

Napton on the Hill

Oxford Canal

PH Rising Sun

① B113

The Folly Inn PH

⑧

② B114

ATB02

③ PB04

⑦ Chapel End

B115 ④ ⑥

Napton Holt

④ PB03

ATB01 B116

⑤

Holt Farm

Oxford Canal

B117

B118

Potash Farm

| 0 | 0.5 | 1.0 | 1.5 miles |

| 0 | 1 | 2 kilometres |

Left: PB03
Stent pillbox.

Right: ATB01
Anti-tank
block.

WALK 2: OXFORD CANAL, NAPTON-ON-THE-HILL	
Distance: 2.5 miles (4km)	**O.S. Map:** Landranger 151: Stratford upon Avon.

Second World War Defence Sites: Two prefabricated pillboxes PB03 and PB04, anti-tank blocks ATB01 and ATB02 and a section of the Oxford Canal, which formed part of the Second World War Southern Command Oxford Canal Stop Line.

Directions to start: Napton-on-the-Hill is 3 miles east of Southam, south of the A425 Southam to Daventry road. The walk start location is at Oxford Canal bridge 113 adjacent to the Folly Inn public house, Folly Lane, south-west of Napton-on-the-Hill. The Folly Inn public house is signposted from the minor road heading south from Napton-on-the-Hill.

Parking: Adjacent to Oxford Canal bridge 113 (NGR 459607). Alternatively, subject to permission, park in the car park of the Folly Inn public house (NGR 457608).

Refreshments: The Folly Inn public house, Napton-on-the-Hill.

The Walk

Note: The walk follows the Oxford Canal towpath, public footpaths and minor roads.

1. From Oxford Canal bridge 113 walk south along the canal towpath to canal bridge 114. *(On the farm track ramp to bridge 114 are two anti-tank blocks ATB02.)*

2. Continue on the towpath past canal bridge 114 to canal Lock No.10. *(Adjacent to canal Lock No.10 and on the opposite side of the canal towpath is Second World War pillbox PB04.)*

3. Continue on the towpath past canal bridge 115. *(Less than 0.5 miles past canal bridge 115 and on the opposite side of the canal towpath is Second World War pillbox PB03.)*

4. Continue on the towpath to canal bridge 116. *(On the approach ramp to canal bridge 116 are two anti-tank blocks ATB01.)*

5. Retrace steps back to canal bridge 115 and exit the canal via a footpath ramp up to the minor road.

6. Cross the canal bridge 115 and within 30m cross the road and enter a field at a gate footpath marker post. Follow the footpath across fields to the minor road at Chapel Green.

7. Turn left at the minor road and walk along the road verge towards Napton-on-the-Hill.

8. Turn left at the second left minor road (Folly Lane) and return to the start at canal bridge 113.

WALK 3 MAP

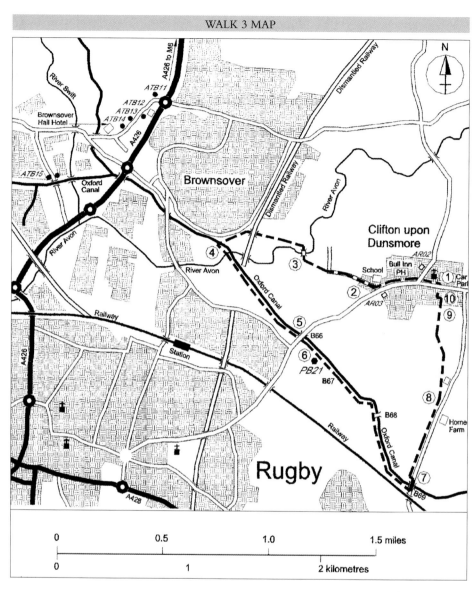

Left: AR02 Air-raid shelter.

Right: PB21 Stent pillbox.

WALK 3: OXFORD CANAL, CLIFTON UPON DUNSMORE	
Distance: 3.5 miles (5.6km)	**O.S. Map:** Landranger 140: Leicester and Coventry area

Second World War Defence Sites: Two air-raid shelters AR02 and AR03, one prefabricated pillbox PB21 and a section of the Oxford Canal, which formed part of the Second World War Western Command Napton to Coventry Stop Line. North of Rugby, but <u>not</u> included on the walk, are anti-tank blocks ATB11 to ATB15. The locations of these ATBs are indicated on the Walk 3 map and can be viewed from public roads.

Directions to start: Clifton upon Dunsmore is 2.5 miles north-east of the centre of Rugby. From Rugby follow the B5414 road to Clifton upon Dunsmore. The walk start location is the free car park adjacent to St Mary's Church, Lilbourne Road, Clifton upon Dunsmore.

Parking: Free car park adjacent to St Mary's Church, Lilbourne Road, Clifton upon Dunsmore.

Refreshments: The Bull Inn public house, Main Street, Clifton upon Dunsmore.

The Walk

Note: The walk follows public footpaths, the Oxford Canal towpath and minor roads.

1. From the free car park adjacent to St Mary's Church walk along Main Street towards Rugby. *(Located in Church Street, to the north of Main Street, is surface air-raid shelter AR02. The shelter is on the west side of Church Street within 100m of the church.)*

2. By the village school, turn right into Station Road and at a sharp right-hand bend enter a field via a stile. Cross the field to a footbridge over the river Avon. *(Located opposite the village school, in South Road, is surface air-raid shelter AR03. The shelter is at the end of a row of terraced houses and is well concealed with ivy.)*

3. From the footbridge turn left, follow the footpath towards Brownsover and walk through an arch under the disused railway embankment (the former Great Central Railway). Bear left and walk to a footpath tunnel under the Oxford Canal.

4. At the exit of the tunnel turn left and walk up the ramp onto the towpath of the Oxford Canal. Turn right and follow the towpath to bridge 66. *(The canal formed part of the Second World War Western Command Stop Line.)*

5. Continue on the towpath past bridge 66. *(Within a 100m past bridge 66 is Second World War pillbox PB21 located in the field close to the towpath.)*

6. Continue on the towpath to bridge 69 and exit the canal via steps up to the minor road.

7. Cross bridge 69 and follow the minor road towards Clifton upon Dunsmore.

8. Shortly past Home Farm leave the road and enter a field, via a stile, on the left-hand side of the road. Follow the signed footpath across fields to Clifton upon Dunsmore, using St Mary's Church tower as a landmark.

9. On reaching Clifton upon Dunsmore follow a signed footpath at the corner of the field passing between two gardens.

10. Turn left at the first road and within 30m turn right along a signed footpath between a bungalow and a house. Continue straight along the footpath to return to Lilbourne Road and the free car park.

WALK 4 MAP

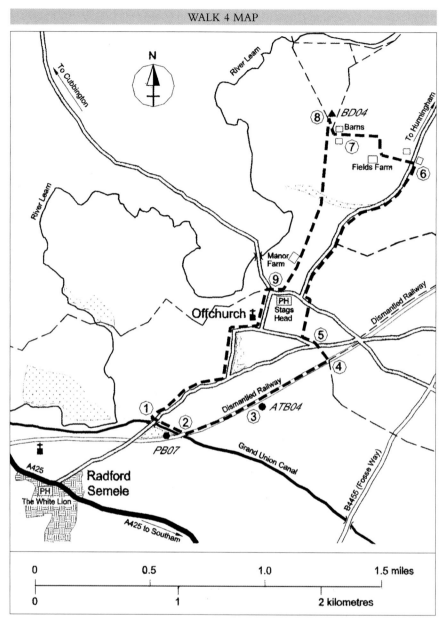

Left: PB07 Type 24 pillbox.

Right: BD04 Bombing decoy shelter.

WALK 4: GRAND UNION CANAL, OFFCHURCH

Distance: 4 miles (6.4km)	**O.S. Map:** Landranger 151: Stratford upon Avon.

Second World War Defence Sites: One pillbox PB07, anti-tank block ATB04, bombing decoy control shelter BD04 and a short section of the Grand Union Canal, which formed part of the Second World War Southern Command Oxford Canal Stop Line.

Directions to start: Offchurch is 3 miles east of the centre of Leamington Spa. From Leamington Spa follow the A425 Southam road. At Radford Semele turn left for Offchurch. The walk start location is at Grand Union Canal bridge 34 located midway between Radford Semele and Offchurch.

Parking: Adjacent to Grand Union Canal bridge 34. (NGR 352650). Alternatively, the walk can be started from Offchurch, with parking in the village or, subject to permission, the car park of the Stag public house (NGR 360659).

Refreshments: The Stag public house, Offchurch.

The Walk

Note: The walk follows the Grand Union Canal towpath, a permitted path along a dismantled railway, public footpaths, a bridleway and minor roads.

1. From Grand Union Canal bridge 34 walk south-east along the canal towpath towards a disused railway viaduct crossing the canal.

2. Walk under the railway viaduct and immediately turn left up a footpath ramp onto the dismantled railway. During 2003 Warwickshire County Council created a new permitted footpath following the route of the dismantled LM&S railway line. *(**Approximately 10m past the opposite end of the disused railway viaduct and on the right-hand side of the dismantled railway is Second World War pillbox PB07. Unfortunately from 2004 the viaduct is no longer a permitted footpath and walkers must not cross the viaduct.**)* From the viaduct continue along the dismantled railway permitted footpath towards the east.

3. Stop where the path dips at a removed bridge crossing a farm track. *(**On the south side anti-tank block ATB04 can be viewed.**)* Continue along the dismantled railway footpath to a bridge crossing the dismantled railway.

4. At the bridge, walk up a footpath ramp onto a farm track. Turn left onto the farm track and walk north towards Offchurch.

5. Cross the minor road and walk along the minor road towards Offchurch. Within 100m and <u>before</u> a thatched cottage, turn right at a signed footpath. On reaching a minor road turn left and within 50m turn right into the minor road signed Hunningham. Continue along this road for almost a mile.

6. At the first group of houses turn left at a signed bridleway to Fields Farm. Bear to the right of Fields Farm, following the bridleway beside a hedgerow.

7. Walk between a group of barns and turn right following the bridle path. *(**Within 100m is bombing decoy control shelter BD04, which formerly housed generators and control equipment for a grid of ground lights and fires acting as a decoy for bombers seeking Coventry**).*

8. Walk back towards the barns and follow a signed footpath across fields, following hedgerows, to Offchurch.

9. The footpath enters Offchurch near the Stag public house. At the road T-junction near the Stag turn left and walk up the hill. Turn right at the T-junction at the top of the hill and follow the minor road signed Leamington Spa to return to the start at bridge 34.

WALK 5 MAP

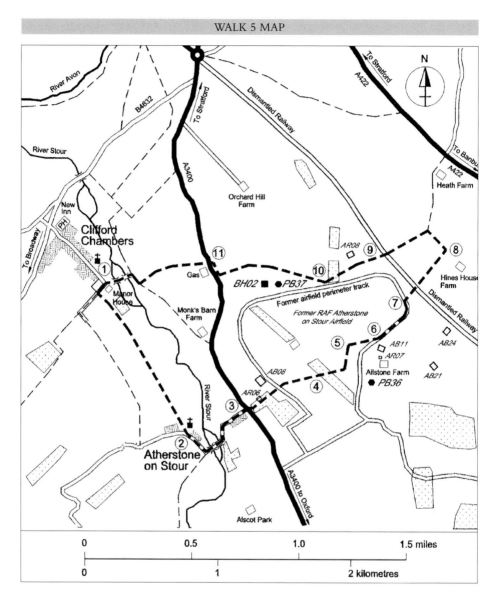

Left: AB11
Control tower.

Right: PB37
Type 24 pillbox.

WALK 5: ATHERSTONE ON STOUR	
Distance: 4.5 miles (7.2km)	**O.S. Map:** Landranger 151: Stratford upon Avon.

Second World War Defence Sites: Former Second World War RAF Stratford Airfield with two pillboxes PB36 and PB37, one battle headquarters BH02, three air-raid shelters AR06 to AR07, shooting range AB24, aircraft hangar AB08, control tower AB11 and other former RAF buildings.

Directions to start: The start location is Clifford Chambers, a village 1 mile south of Stratford-upon-Avon on the B4632 road. When approaching from Stratford-upon-Avon on the B4632 road turn left into the village by the New Inn public house.

Parking: In the main street of Clifford Chambers near to the church (NGR 198521). Alternatively for a shorter walk parking is available in the side road at the A3400 road junction to Atherstone on Stour (NGR 209511).

Refreshments: The New Inn, Clifford Chambers.

The Walk

Note: Part of the walk follows public footpaths across the former RAF Stratford Airfield. The various Second World War defences are located on private farmland. These defences can viewed from the public footpaths and walkers must not stray off the footpaths onto private land.

1. Walk down the main street and turn right at a farm track in front of Clifford Manor House. Within 50m turn left at a footpath junction and follow the footpath across fields to Atherstone on Stour.

2. At Atherstone on Stour turn left on to the minor road and continue to the A3400 main road via a road bridge over the river Stour.

3. Cross the A3400 road and follow the signed footpath through a small wood. *(**Within the woods are derelict RAF buildings including a derelict Stanton air-raid shelter AR06.**)* Pass to the right of a *former aircraft hangar* *(**AB08**)* and follow the signed footpath across fields to a narrow wood.

4. Walk through the wood and cross the fields with Ailstone Farm to the east. *(**From the footpath crossing the first field pillbox PB36 can be viewed in the distance, to the south of Ailstone Farm.**)*

5. Follow the signed footpath to the north of Ailstone Farm. *(**Adjacent to Ailstone Farm is a Second World War RAF control tower building AB11.**)*

6. The public footpath follows the route of the former RAF airfield perimeter track.

7. Shortly after a left-hand bend on the perimeter track, turn right onto a signed footpath. *(**To the south-west in the distance can be seen a derelict RAF shooting range AB24 and the mound of a derelict bomb store AB21.**)* The footpath crosses the dismantled Midland Railway and continues across fields adjacent to a fence.

8. Turn left near Hines House Farm and within 100m turn left and follow the footpath adjacent to a fence to return to the dismantled railway.

9. Cross the open fields to a small wood. *(**In the middle of the first field is a derelict RAF Stanton air-raid shelter AR08.**)*

10. Follow the signed footpath through the wood, cross a field and follow the footpath beside a hedgerow. *(**To the south in the middle of the field Second World War pillbox PB37 and battle headquarters BH02 can be seen.**)*

11. At the A3400 road turn right. Within 100m turn left at a signed footpath (adjacent to a gas booster station) and return to Clifford Chambers via footbridges over the river Stour.

Appendix 4

Timeline for Twentieth-Century Defences in Warwickshire

WARWICKSHIRE EVENTS	NATIONAL AND WORLDWIDE EVENTS
	1901 – Queen Victoria's death
	1904–1905 – Russo-Japanese War
1912 – Castle Bromwich Airfield established	
	1914 – Outbreak of the First World War
1916 – Lilbourne Airfield used for fighter aircraft	
1917 – Radford Airfield opened	
1918 – Whitley Airfield opened	**1918 (11 November)** – First World War Armistice signed
1919 – Lilbourne Airfield closed	**1919 (15 June)** – First aeroplane crossing of the Atlantic
1920 – Warwickshire Yeomanry re-formed	
1926 – Rugby Radio Station operational	
1926 – RAF Castle Bromwich opened	**1926** – General Strike in Britain
	1933 – Hitler appointed Chancellor of Germany
	1934 – Death of Hindenburg. Hitler becomes dictator
1937 (12 April) – Whittle tests the gas turbine jet engine	
	1939 (1 September) – Germany invades Poland

WARWICKSHIRE EVENTS	NATIONAL AND WORLDWIDE EVENTS
1939 – RAF Elmdon opened	**1939 (3 September)** – Britain and France declare war on Germany
1940 – RAF bases opened at Ansty, Baginton, Bramcote and Southam	**1940 (10 May)** – Winston Churchill becomes Prime Minister
1940 (14 November) – Coventry Blitz, Moonlight Sonata	
1941 – RAF bases opened at Brinklow, Church Lawford, Hockley Heath, Honiley, Leamington Spa, Long Marston, Wellesbourne Mountford, Stratford and Warwick	**1941 (22 June)** – Germany invades Russia
	1941 (7 December) – Japan attacks US fleet at Pearl Harbor
	1941 (8 December) – USA and UK declare war on Japan
1942 – RAF Gaydon opened	**1942 (4 November)** – British victory at El Alamein
1943 – RAF Snitterfield opened	**1943 (3 September)** – Allied invasion of Italy
1944 – RAF Southam closed	**1944 (6 June)** – D-Day landings in Normandy
1945 – RAF bases closed at Baginton, Brinklow, Hockley Heath, Leamington Spa, Stratford and Warwick	**1945 (8 May)** – End of Second World War in Europe
	1945 (6 and 8 August) – Atomic bombs dropped on Japan
	1945 (14 August) – Japan surrenders
1946 – RAF bases closed at Elmdon and Snitterfield.	
1946 – RAF Bramcote becomes RNAS HMS *Gamecock*	
	1949 (4 April) – North Atlantic Treaty signed
	1950 (25 June) – Korean War begins
	1952 (3 October) – First British atomic bomb detonated at north-western Australia test area
	1952 (1 November) – First US hydrogen bomb detonated
1953 – RAF Ansty closed	**1953 (12 August)** – First Russian hydrogen bomb detonated
1954 – RAF Long Marston closed	
1955 (January) – The Valiant, the first of the new V-bombers, enters service at RAF Gaydon	
1955 – RAF Church Lawford closed	**1956 (May)** – The Vulcan V-bomber enters service at RAF Waddington
	1956 (11 October) – First British nuclear bomb (Yellow Sun) dropped over southern Australia test area

WARWICKSHIRE EVENTS	NATIONAL AND WORLDWIDE EVENTS
	1956 (31 October) – Suez Crisis begins
1957 (November) – The Victor V-bomber enters service at RAF Gaydon	**1957 (15 May)** – First British Hydrogen bomb (Blue Danube) dropped near Christmas Island test area
1958 – RAF bases closed at Castle Bromwich and Honiley	
1959 – RNAS HMS *Gamecock* becomes Gamecock Barracks	**1959** – Thor missiles deployed in Britain
1960 (10 August) – Budbrooke Barracks closed at Warwick	
	1961 (August) – Berlin wall constructed
	1962 (October) – Cuban missile crisis
1963 – RAF Wellesbourne Mountford closed	**1963 (February)** – British Blue Steel missile enters service
1968 – Cold War ROC underground monitoring posts closed at Alderminster, Henley-in-Arden, Harbury, Napton-on-the-Hill and Curdworth.	**1968** – Royal Observer Corps reduced in size
	1972 (26 May) – SALT 1 agreement signed
1974 – RAF Gaydon closed	
	1982 (April to June) – Falklands War against Argentina
	1987 (8 December) – Intermediate Nuclear Forces Treaty signed by USA and USSR
	1989 (11 November) – Fall of the Berlin Wall
	1990 (3 October) – Germany reunified
1991 – Cold War ROC underground monitoring posts closed at Long Compton, Bidford-on-Avon, Edgehill, Barford, Haseley Knob, Bedworth, Meriden, Shirley and Erdington	**1991 (June)** – RAF Greenham Common cruise missile facility stood down
	1991 (31 July) – START 1 treaty signed
	1991 (September) – Royal Observer Corps disbanded
	1991 (26 December) – USSR dissolved
1992 – ROC group headquarters bunker closed at Lawford Heath	
1999 (1 April) – Royal Engineers Long Marston Depot vacated by MoD	

Appendix 5

Defences Study Groups

Readers wishing to obtain further information on twentieth-century defences, pillboxes and fortifications are recommended to join the following study groups:

Pillbox Study Group (PSG)

The Pillbox Study Group (PSG) is a research group run by volunteers and has been established for over ten years. PSG members receive an informative journal, *Loopholes*, three times a year, detailing finds and sites of particular interest to the military archaeologist.

Details on how to join the PSG are provided on the PSG website.

The PSG website (**www.pillbox-study-group.org.uk**) is regularly updated and provides excellent information on pillboxes and Second World War defences. The website also provides links to other websites relating to pillboxes and defences.

The PSG official handbook, *British Anti-Invasion Defences 1940–1945*, provides a very good overview of Second World War defences and is published by the Historic Military Press.

Fortress Study Group (FSG)

The Fortress Study Group (FSG) is an international society concerned with the study of all aspects of military architecture and fortifications and their armaments, especially works constructed to mount and resist artillery. The group was founded in 1975 at Pembroke College, Oxford.

The FSG holds an annual conference each September over a long weekend with visits and evening lectures, an annual tour abroad lasting about eight days, and an annual Members Day.

The FSG journal, *Fort*, is published annually and the FSG newsletter magazine, *Casemate*, is published three times a year.

Membership is international and open to every individual or institution with an active interest in the study, protection and preservation of all aspects of fortifications and their armaments of all periods.

Details on how to join the FSG are provided on the FSG website (**www.fsgfort.com**) or contact: The Secretary, c/o 6 Lanark Place, London W9 1BS.

Appendix 6

Abbreviations

AA	Anti-aircraft artillery		ESH	Explosives Store House
AAOR	Anti-aircraft Operations Room		FG	Fighter Group
AB	Airfield Building		FSG	Fortress Study Group
ABD	Army Barracks & Depot		FTS	Flying Training School
ADGB	Air Defence of Great Britain		FW	Fortifications and Works
AGS	Air Gunners School			
ALG	Advanced Landing Ground		GCHQ	Government Communications HQ
AM	Air Ministry		GDA	Gun Defended Area (Anti-aircraft)
AML	Air Ministry Laboratory		GHQ	General Headquarters
AR	Air Raid			
APB	Ammunition Process Building		HAA	Heavy Anti-aircraft
ARP	Air-Raid Precautions		HF	High Frequency
ASU	Aircraft Storage Unit		HG	Home Guard
AT	Anti-tank			
ATB	Anti-tank Block		ICBM	Inter-continental Ballistic Missile
AWA	Armstrong-Whitworth Aircraft			
			LAA	Light Anti-aircraft
BAD	Base Ammunition Depot		LDV	Local Defence Volunteers
BD	Bombing Decoy			
BG	Bombardment Group		MoD	Ministry of Defence
BH	Battle Headquarters		MoS	Ministry of Supply
BHQ	Battle Headquarters		MoW	Ministry of Works
			MT	Motor Transport
CAD	Central Ammunition Depot		MU	Maintenance Unit
CEP	Central Engineering Park			
CFS	Central Flying School		OP	Observation Post
CND	Campaign for Nuclear Disarmament		OTU	Operational Training Unit
CRC	Camp Reception Centre			
CRS	Carrier Repeater Station		PB	Pillbox
CW	Cold War		PBX	Private Branch Exchange
			PW	Prisoner of War
DL	Defended Locality		PoW	Prisoner of War
DMC	Defence Munitions Centre		PR	Photographic Reconnaissance
DoB	Defence of Britain Project		PSG	Pillbox Study Group
DZ	Drop Zone			
			RAE	Royal Aircraft Establishment
ELG	Emergency Landing Ground		RAF	Royal Air Force

RC	Reinforced Concrete		TA	Territorial Army
RDF	Radio Direction Finding		TTE	Telephone Trunk Exchange
RE	Royal Engineers			
RLG	Relief Landing Ground		UESH	Underground Explosives Store House
RNVR	Royal Naval Volunteer Reserve		UKWMO	United Kingdom Warning and Monitoring Organisation
ROC	Royal Observer Corps			
RSG	Regional Seat of Government		UMP	Underground Monitoring Post
RSJ	Rolled Steel Joist			
			VHF	Very High Frequency
SESH	Standard Explosives Store House		VP	Vulnerable Point
SF	Starfish (Bombing decoy site)		VR	Voluntary Reserve
SL	Searchlight			
SLG	Satellite Landing Ground		W/T	Wireless Telegraphy
SRHQ	Sub-regional Headquarters			
SRSG	Sub-regional Seat of Government			
START	Strategic Arms Reduction Talks			

Bibliography

General Defences Books

Ironside's Line, Colin Alexander, ISBN: 1 901313 04 2
Silent Sentinels (The story of Norfolk's fixed defences during the twentieth century), Christopher Bird, ISBN: 0 948400 81 1
Stronghold – A History of Military Architecture, Martin H. Brace, ISBN: 0 7134 4356 1
20th Century Defences in Britain – Kent, David Burridge, ISBN: 1 85753 233 3
Beaches, Fields, Streets, and Hills: The Anti-Invasion Landscapes of England 1940, William Foot, ISBN: 1 902771 53 2
The Battlefields That Nearly Were: Defended England 1940, William Foot, ISBN: 0 7524 3849 2
War Walks Stop Line Green, Maj. M. Green, ISBN: 1 873877 39 0
Leamington's Czech Patriots and the Heydrich Assassination, Alan Griffin, ISBN: 0 9514478 3 1
British Home Defences 1940–45, Bernard Lowry, ISBN: 1841767670
20th Century Defences in Britain – An Introductory Guide, Council for British Archaeology (CBA), Editor: Bernard Lowry, ISBN: 1 872414 57 5
Discovering Fortifications from the Tudors to the Cold War, Bernard Lowry, ISBN: 0 7478 0651 9
Frontline Sussex – The Defence Lines of West Sussex 1939–1945, Martin Mace, ISBN: 1 901313 00 X
Sussex Wartime Relics and Memorials, Martin Mace, ISBN: 1 901313 01 8
Always Ready – The Drill Halls of Britain's Volunteer Forces, Dr Mike Osbourne, ISBN: 1 85818 509 2
Defending Britain; 20th Century Military Structures in the Landscape, Dr Mike Osbourne, ISBN: 0 7524 3134 X
20th Century Defences in Britain – Cambridgeshire, Dr Mike Osbourne, ISBN: 0 9540378 0 4
20th Century Defences in Britain – Lincolnshire, Dr Mike Osbourne, ISBN: 1 85753 267 8
20th Century Defences in Britain – The East Midlands, Dr Mike Osbourne, ISBN: 0 95403781 2
20th Century Defences in Britain – The London Area, Dr Mike Osbourne, ISBN: 0 95403780 5
British Anti-Invasion Defences 1940–1945 (the official handbook of the Pillbox Study Group), Austin Ruddy, ISBN: 1 901313 20 4
Fortress Britain, A. Saunders, ISBN: 1 85512 000 3
Resisting the Nazi Invader, Arthur Ward, ISBN: 0 09476 750 5
Stronghold Britain – Four Thousand Years of British Fortifications, Geoffrey Williams, ISBN: 0 7509 1554 4
Pillboxes – A Study of UK Defences 1940, Henry Wills, ISBN: 0 436 57360 1

Journals and Periodicals

Loopholes, Pillbox Study Group (PSG)
Fort and *Casemate*, Fortress Study Group (FSG)

RAF Airfield and Aviation Books

Whittle 1907–1996: Warwickshire's Genius of the Jet, Paul Bolitho, Warwickshire County Council

World War 2 Airfields, Philip Birtles, ISBN: 0 7110 2681 5

Action Stations: 6. Military Airfields of the Cotswolds and the Central Midlands, Michael J.F. Bowyer, ISBN: 1 85260 372 0

British Airfield Buildings of the Second World War, Graham Buchan-Innes, ISBN: 1 85780 026 5

British Airfield Buildings of the Second World War; Volume 2: The Expansion & Inter-War Periods, Graham Buchan-Innes, ISBN: 1 85780 101 6

Fields of Deception: Britain's Bombing Decoys of World War 2, Colin Dobinson, ISBN: 0 413 745708

A.A. Command: Britain's Anti-aircraft Defences of the Second World War, Colin Dobinson, ISBN: 0 413 765407

British Military Airfield Architecture, Paul Francis, ISBN: 1 85260 462 x

Angry Skies across the Vale (RAF Honeybourne and RAF Long Marston), Brian Kedward, ISBN: 0 9527002 0 4

Air Raid – The Bombing of Coventry 1940, Norman Longmate, ISBN: 0 09 920850 4

Blitz on Britain 1939–45, Alfred Price, ISBN: 0 7509 2356 3

Britain's Military Airfields 1939–45, David J. Smith, ISBN: 1 852060 038 1

Warwickshire Airfields in the Second World War, Graham Smith, ISBN: 1 85306 867 5

Propellers over Warwick, Midland Warplane Museum 1991

Cold War Defences Books

Cold War Building for Nuclear Confrontation 1946–1989, Wayne D. Cocroft and Roger J.C. Thomas, ISBN: 1 873592 81 7

Four Minute Warning; Britain's Cold War, Bob Clarke, ISBN: 0 7524 3394 6

Cold War Secret Nuclear Bunkers, N.J. McCamley, ISBN: 0 85052 945 X

Secret Underground Cities, N.J. McCamley, ISBN: 0 85052 733 3

Attack Warning Red: The Royal Observer Corps and the Defence of Britain 1925 to 1975, Derek Wood, ISBN: 0356 08411 6

Websites

Pillbox Study Group website (www.pillbox-study-group.org.uk), Graham Matthews (Pillbox Study Group)

Fortress Study Group (www.fsgfort.com)

Defence of Britain website (www.britarch.ac.uk/projects/dob), Council for British Archaeology (CBA)

Defence of Britain database (www.ads.ahds.ac.uk/catalogue/resources.html/dob), Council for British Archaeology (CBA)

Warwickshire Sites and Monuments Record (www.warwickshire.gov.uk/timetrail), Warwickshire County Council

Tim Carter's pillboxes website (www.geocities.com/pentagon/camp/3224/), Tim Carter

Ian Sanders pillboxes website (www.uk.geocities.com/pillboxesuk), Ian Sanders

Somerset pillboxes website (www.somersetpillboxes.co.uk), David Tacchi

Subterranea Britannica (www.subbrit.org.uk), Subterranea Britannica

Airfield Research Group (www.airfield-reseach-group.co.uk), Airfield Research Group

World War Two Airfields (www.worldwar2airfields.fotopic.net), World War Two Airfields Group

Air Atlantique Classic Flight (www.classicflight.com), Air Atlantique Classic Flight, Coventry Airport

Index

If you are interested in purchasing other books published by Tempus,
or in case you have difficulty finding any Tempus books in your local bookshop,
you can also place orders directly through our website

www.tempus-publishing.com